Hiking
Colorado's
Weminuche
Wilderness

Donna Lynn Ikenberry

FALCON®

HELENA, MONTANA

Falcon® Publishing is continually expanding its list of recreation guidebooks. All books include detailed descriptions, accurate maps, and all the information necessary for enjoyable trips. You can order extra copies of this book and get information and prices for other Falcon® books by writing Falcon, P.O. Box 1718, Helena, Montana 59624 or calling toll free 1-800-582-2665. Also, please ask for a free copy of our current catalog. Visit our website at www.FalconOutdoors.com or contact us by e-mail at falcon@falcon.com.

©1999 Falcon® Publishing, Inc., Helena, Montana
Printed in the United States of America.

2 3 4 5 6 7 8 9 0 MG 04 03 02 01 00

Falcon and FalconGuide are registered trademarks of Falcon® Publishing, Inc.

Library of Congress Cataloging-in-Publication Data

Ikenberry, Donna Lynn.
    Hiking Colorado's Weminuche Wilderness / Donna Lynn Ikenberry.
        p.   cm. — (A FalconGuide)
    Includes bibliographical references (p.   ) and index.
    ISBN 1-56044-716-8 (pbk.)
    1. Hiking—Colorado—Weminuche Wilderness—Guidebooks. 2. Trails—
Colorado—Weminuche Wilderness—Guidebooks. 3. Weminuche
Wilderness (Colo.)—Guidebooks. I. Title. II. Series: Falcon
guide.
GV199.42.C62W465   1999
796.51'09788'38—dc21   98-55765
                                                                CIP

CAUTION

Outdoor recreational activities are by their very nature potentially hazardous. All participants in such activities must assume the responsibility for their own actions and safety. The information contained in this guidebook cannot replace sound judgment and good decision-making skills, which help reduce risk exposure, nor does the scope of this book allow for disclosure of all the potential hazards and risks involved in such activities.

Learn as much as possible about the outdoor recreational activities in which you participate, prepare for the unexpected, and be cautious. The reward will be a safer and more enjoyable experience.

♻ Text pages printed on recycled paper.

For my best friend and fiancé, Mike Vining

(Donna and Mike got married January 6, 1999,
on top of Mauna Kea, Hawaii's highest point.)

Contents

Continental Divide Trail

Acknowledgments

I have explored the vast and lovely Weminuche Wilderness alone on many occasions. I thank God every day for allowing me to see and feel places like the Weminuche: to experience its explosive grandeur above timberline; to delight in a tiny wildflower growing miraculously out of hardened granite; to smile at the sound of bugling elk.

Though I hiked alone much of the time, I was fortunate to have company now and then. Carol Kaufman joined me sometimes, adding joy to every journey with intense discussions about literature and life. Michelle DeLaria met me for two backpack trips, keeping me warm when hypothermia threatened to set in during one cold deluge. I am indebted to her—not only did we have a great time, she probably saved my life. I made some new friends along the way, too. Nancy and Jim Haynes shuttled me some, with Nancy joining me for two fun-filled day hikes. In addition, I introduced Johnna Heberling to backpacking with a two-day backpack up Squaw Creek.

What I didn't know my first season in the Weminuche was that the next season I would come back engaged to my best friend, Mike Vining. This book is dedicated to my future husband, the kindest, nicest, and most thoughtful, respectful, truthful, and generous man I have ever known and loved. A special thanks goes to him; he made the Continental Divide Trail so very special. I also want to express my gratitude to his Aunt Audrey and Uncle Ray Vining. They shuttled us to Wolf Creek Pass, making our long hike possible.

Although my family isn't into hiking and backpacking, they are forever in my heart and thoughts as I walk trails. My parents, Donald and Beverly Ikenberry, bless me with their love, support, and readiness always to believe in me. My two brothers and their families offer the same. I am proud to have Don Ikenberry and his wife, Yolie Gutierrez, in my life. I'm equally blessed with David Ikenberry, his wife Laura, and my niece and nephew, Sarah and Andrew. New family additions include my new "daughter" Terri Vining and her son Mitchell, my other new "daughter" Lorri Sturdavant and her son, Dillon, and my "mom" and "dad," Roger and Arlene Vining.

I have many other friends (some of whom are like family) to thank. Although you are too numerous to mention, you know who you are. You are often in my thoughts and always in my prayers.

I must acknowledge several outdoor companies that provided everything from pedometers, hiking boots, backpacks, day pack, tent, and waterproof jackets and pants to cold-weather mitts. Thank you Avocet, Coleman, Columbia Sportswear, Danner, Hi-Tec, Jansport, Kelty, Nikwax, North Face, Outdoor Research, Precise International, Performance, and Solstice.

Working on this book, I based myself in several communities and want to thank those who helped me there. Patti Zink, of the Durango Area Chamber Resort Association, arranged for complimentary train tickets from the

Durango & Silverton Narrow Gauge Railroad, and complimentary lodging at the Durango KOA East. While I was living in South Fork for two months, Roy Snyder allowed me to use his computer (and Internet connection) so I could keep up with my e-mail. He and his wife Sandra asked that I give thanks to them in memory of their daughter Sonni, who died in May 1998. In South Fork I had the sweetest, kindest neighbors. A special thank you goes to Linda and Jerry Tullos and the rest of the gang at the South Fork Campground.

In addition, I asked for and received information and other necessary help from both the San Juan and Rio Grande National Forests. Special thanks go to the personnel who read and checked my manuscript: Peggy Jacobson, Phyllis Wong Decker, and Ron Decker at the Pagosa Ranger District; Randy Houtz, Bayfield Ranger District; and Jody Fairchild, Divide Ranger District.

I send a sincere blessing to David Lee, my guidebook editor, and all the other good folks at Falcon Publishing. Thanks once more for a job well done.

Topo Map

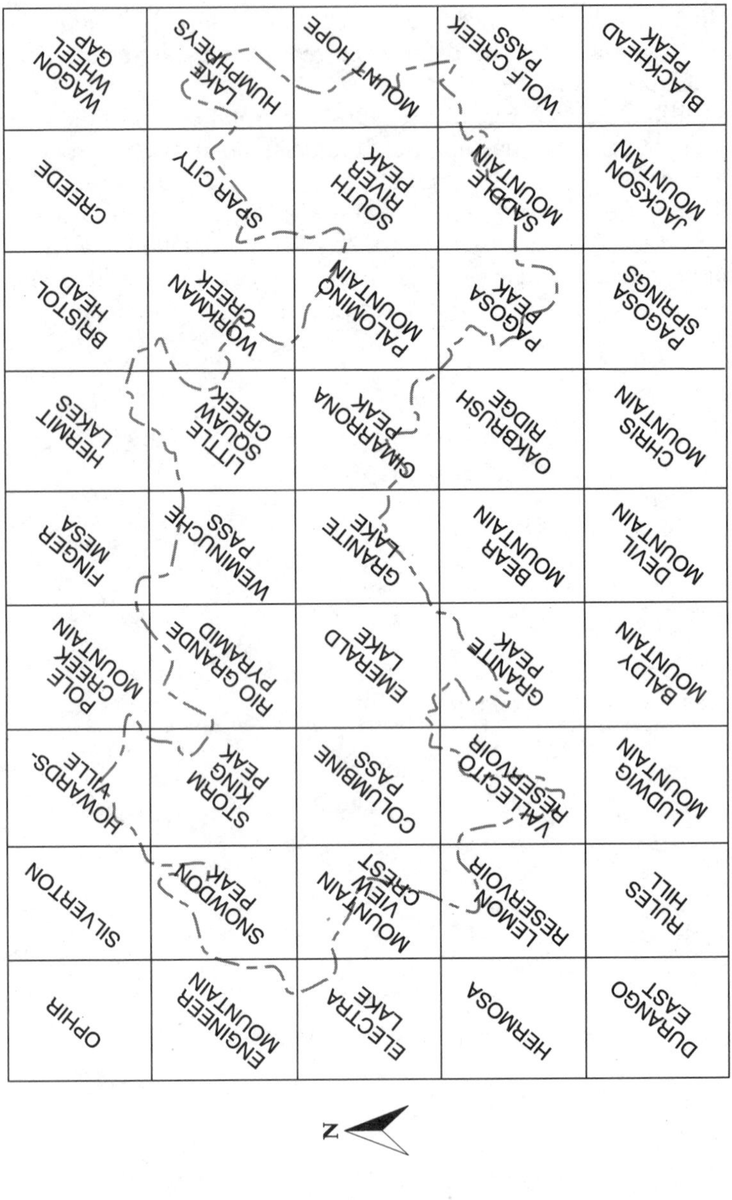
WAGON WHEEL GAP
LAKE HUMPHREYS
MOUNT HOPE
WOLF CREEK PASS
BLACKHEAD PEAK
CREEDE
SPAR CITY
SOUTH RIVER PEAK
SADDLE MOUNTAIN
JACKSON MOUNTAIN
BRISTOL HEAD
WORKMAN CREEK
PALOMINO MOUNTAIN
PAGOSA PEAK
PAGOSA SPRINGS
HERMIT LAKES
LITTLE SQUAW CREEK
CIMARRONA PEAK
OAKBRUSH RIDGE
CHRIS MOUNTAIN
FINGER MESA
WEMINUCHE PASS
GRANITE LAKE
BEAR MOUNTAIN
DEVIL MOUNTAIN
POLE CREEK MOUNTAIN
RIO GRANDE PYRAMID
EMERALD LAKE
GRANITE PEAK
BALDY MOUNTAIN
HOWARDS-VILLE
STORM KING PEAK
COLUMBINE PASS
VALLECITO RESERVOIR
LUDWIG MOUNTAIN
SILVERTON
SNOWDON PEAK
MOUNTAIN VIEW CREST
LEMON RESERVOIR
RULES HILL
OPHIR
ENGINEER MOUNTAIN
ELECTRA LAKE
HERMOSA
DURANGO EAST
N

Overview Map

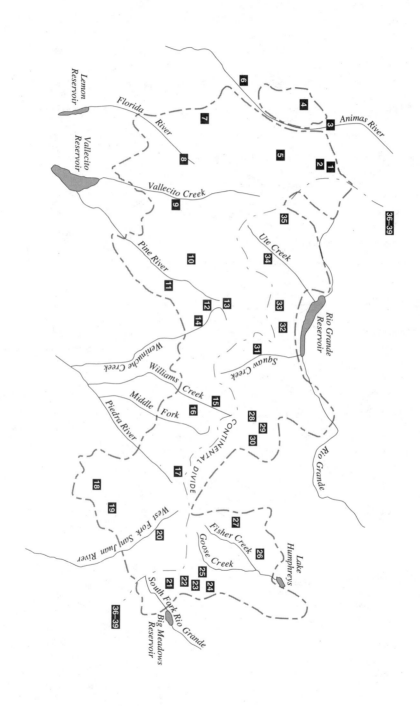

Map Legend

Interstate

U.S. Highway

State or Other
Principal Road

Interstate Highway

Paved Road

Gravel Road

Unimproved Road

Trailhead

Main Trail(s)/Route(s)

Alternate/Secondary
Trail(s)/Route(s)

River/Creek

Spring

Campground

Cabins/Buildings

Peak
9,782 ft.

Elevation
9,782 ft.

Pass

Overlook/Point
of Interest

National Forest/Park
Boundary

Map Orientation
N

Scale
0   0.5   1
Miles

Introduction

It is a place of see-forever views, a place where waves of mountains rush to the horizon. It is a place where peaks stretch into the heavens; at times I'm convinced that their lofty tips touch the sky. It is a place where coyotes yelp in wildflower-blessed meadows, and snowshoe rabbits scamper down willow-lined trails. It holds a mix of summer and winter, of soft brown bodies and snow white feet. On its silent lakes beavers slap at sunset, and black bears roam through its lush forests. It is a place where elk herds tiptoe quietly through woods or congregate in meadows, feeding while hikers watch from a ridge above.

It is the Weminuche Wilderness.

Tucked away in Colorado's southwest corner, the Weminuche (pronounced WHEM-a-nooch) Wilderness encompasses 499,771 acres. Named for a band of Ute Indians who lived, hunted, fished in, and honored the spirit of this stunning land, the area was first designated a wilderness in 1975. When asked exactly where this diverse wilderness area is located, I always tell folks it's easy to find: just get a map and look for the quaint towns of Durango, Silverton, Creede, South Fork, and Pagosa Springs, then connect the dots of these towns. The Weminuche is smack-dab in the center, in the heart of the stunning San Juan Mountains.

With an average elevation of 10,000 feet, the Weminuche is probably one of the highest wilderness areas in the nation. It is Colorado's largest and most popular wilderness area. Average elevation at most of the trailheads is a mind-boggling 9,000 feet—and that's only the beginning. Hike or backpack from one of the trailheads and you can find yourself walking a ridge at 12,000 feet or more, with 13,000- and 14,000-foot peaks surrounding you.

Looking for a 13,000-foot peak to scale? High peaks are more than plentiful here. From almost any lofty point you'll see waves of them to the west, north, east, and south. Three of Colorado's 54 "Fourteeners," as they are known, grace the wilderness: Mount Eolus (14,083 feet), Sunlight Peak (14,059 feet), and Windom Peak (14,082 feet). All three peaks are popular climbs. In fact, there are so many high-elevation peaks in the Weminuche that many of them are yet unnamed.

In addition to peaks, the wilderness contains 81 high mountain lakes, numerous streams and creeks, and the headwaters of five rivers—the Animas, Los Pinos (the Pines), the Piedra, the Rio Grande, and the San Juan. The region is jointly managed by the San Juan and Rio Grande National Forests. Thirty-one trailheads provide access to the many trails that dissect the wilderness. There are 490 miles of managed trails, countless miles of non-managed trails, and abundant opportunities to bushwhack wherever your heart and feet lead you. In addition to driving to the trailhead of your choice, you can also access the Chicago Basin and Elk Park region via a narrow-gauge train, which runs from Durango to Silverton and back again.

Mike Vining on the Continental Divide Trail near the East Ute Creek Trail.

If you have time and you like high-elevation trails, you'll want to hike the Continental Divide Trail. This long-distance trail stretches more than 3,000 miles, from Antelope Wells, New Mexico, to Waterton, Alberta. The trail crosses the Continental Divide 475 times along its route. More than 80 miles of the trail pass through the Weminuche. The 469-mile Colorado Trail also passes through the northwest corner of the wilderness.

The Weminuche is Colorado's most popular wilderness, but you can still find solitude here if that's what you're looking for. In this FalconGuide, I've noted which trails are heavily used (see "Trail conditions" in each entry) so that you can avoid them. If you want to explore a place that gets heavy use, try visiting on a non-holiday weekday, or early or late in the season.

I spent two wonderful summers hiking many of the trails in the Weminuche Wilderness. I chose distinct paths through diverse country. My goal was to best showcase the wilderness, something I needn't have bothered to do. After hiking about 700 miles of wilderness trails, I've come to the conclusion that the Weminuche is its own best showcase.

Although I tended to stay away from overcrowded areas, I do describe some heavily used areas in this guide. Why? If I didn't, you'd think I had forgotten them. Because of their renowned beauty, I just had to see some of these places for myself. I hiked the Needle Creek and Elk Creek Trails, two of the most heavily used paths in the wilderness. I did it over the July 4th holiday and managed to camp alone every single night. To do so, I dropped off Columbine Pass and descended into the higher portion of the Chicago Basin as most folks were heading out. I camped there for two nights, with the nearest backpacker about half a mile away. Hiking out, I saw people crammed together, camping too close to the water, blatantly disturbing the land. I was glad I had stayed up high, keeping the splendid view of the lovely 14,000-footers and other lofty peaks all to myself.

Although both of these often-visited places were as stunning as I'd heard, I have seen other jewels in the Weminuche that were equally exquisite. I recommend leaving Needle Creek and Elk Creek to the crowds, taking off on your own instead on some lonely trail. Look in the southern, eastern, and northern reaches of the wilderness for a more solitary experience. See Appendix D for additional suggestions. Happy hiking!

HOW TO USE THIS GUIDE

In this book I describe several types of hikes, including both day hikes and extended backpack trips. You'll find everything from one-way hikes (begin at one trailhead, hike in, and return to the same trailhead on the same trail), semi-loop hikes (begin and end on the same trail, hiking at least one other trail along the way), and loop hikes (follow two trails that loop together and meet at the same place) to shuttle-loops (begin and end the hike at two separate trailheads—requiring a shuttle in between).

Of course, you can always mix and match hikes to fit personal likes and dislikes. For instance, though I've written about the Turkey Creek and West Fork San Juan Trails individually, it's easy to combine the two if you have access to a shuttle. The Kitty Creek and Hope Creek Trails make a nice loop—you can walk from one trailhead to the other. If you're interested in a short day hike, of which there are few in this wilderness, you can always follow the trail description for one of the longer day hikes or extended backpack trips. Just hike out as far as you want, enjoy the area, then head back to the trailhead.

I have given each trail a **difficulty rating**, something that isn't always easy to do. How does a person judge the difficulty of one trail over another? A trail that seems easy to me may seem moderately difficult to you. I've hiked trails that seemed moderate one day, and steep the next. My physical condition, the type of day I'm having, and even the weather play roles in judging what's hard and what's not. It's also hard to pinpoint a rating for a trail that is less than a mile long but very steep. Should it be rated easy, because it's short, or strenuous, because it's steep? Some trails are easy in some sections, then downright strenuous in other portions. I've taken all that into consideration.

Trails in this guide are rated as easy, moderate, or strenuous. An **easy** hike is usually on a shorter trail, with gentle grades. It may be nearly flat. **Moderate** hikes are longer, but usually less than 8 miles round-trip. Elevation gains on these routes are usually no more than 500 feet per mile. Hikes rated **strenuous** are usually longer than 8 miles and have steep gains and descents. These are the thigh-pounders and calf-busters. Please note: Some difficult trails are short, but steep and strenuous!

You'll find **elevation graphs** for each of the hikes in this guide. Highly useful, these graphs show the rate at which you will ascend or descend to a given destination. Please remember that short climbs and drops will not appear here, because of the small scale of the maps. Information given in the text should eliminate any surprises.

Although I've also provided a location **map**, I recommend using either the Trails Illustrated Weminuche Wilderness map or one of the United States Geological Survey (USGS) maps listed under the "Maps" section of each trail description. Topographic maps are highly useful because they show the surface configuration of the land. In addition to showing natural features such as lakes, rivers, streams, and forests, they allow you to tell where the land is flat and where it is steep. On such maps, contour lines that are close together indicate that the land is steep.

After a general description about the trails—including their highlights, popularity, length, difficulty, elevation, related map, and so on—each **hike description** furnishes you with all the information you'll need to find Weminuche trailheads and hike the wilderness trails. I've also included information about trailhead facilities and locations of the nearest campgrounds. Read on to find tips on trail etiquette, information on the seasons and weather, a special section for hiking with children, tips on minimum-impact hiking and camping, a brief section on the natural history of the region, and a whole lot more.

Most of the trails have names, and some have numbers too. I've described all of the trails by name, but if the Forest Service has given the trail a number then I've listed that in the text as well. In addition, I've described signs along the trail, telling you what the signs say so you can better stay on the correct trail.

BEING PREPARED: BACKCOUNTRY ESSENTIALS AND SAFETY

Just like the outside world, the backcountry is wrought with danger. Mostly, it's dangerous for those who enter the wilderness without being ready for it. These folks tackle the outdoors as they would tackle any other situation in life, forgetting that you can't fight Mother Nature—and if you do, you definitely won't win.

Always enter the backcountry properly prepared. Carry equipment and clothing to suit the altitude, climate, and any sudden change in weather you might encounter. In high-elevation areas such as the Weminuche, you should always dress in layers. Pack enough food and water for your trip, even if it's just a day hike. In addition, always take along a space blanket and a first-aid kit for emergencies. Overnight backpackers will need to carry essential camping equipment, enough food for the length of the trip, and so on. Appendix C lists suggested equipment for hikes of all lengths.

Regardless of whether you hike alone or with a friend, leave a detailed itinerary with someone before you head out, listing trails you plan to hike and the date you plan to return. I always leave my parents' and my fiancé's telephone numbers in case of an emergency. If I am injured or get really sick and have to be rescued, I don't have to worry about paying the cost; I purchased a Colorado Hiker's Certificate. Issued by the Colorado Division of Wildlife, this certificate is good for rescue anywhere in the state. Created in 1995, it helps fund search-and-rescue efforts, and contributes to Colorado's non-game and endangered animals funds. (A Colorado hunting and fishing license automatically provides the same coverage.) Colorado Hiking Certificates are available at all Colorado Division of Wildlife offices, and at most outdoor sports stores.

You can avoid a possible rescue by being cautious. Be careful glissading down steep snowfields, don't climb rock faces without ropes, and ford creeks that are below your ability, not above it. If you're hiking in a group, be courteous, and slow your pace down to that of the slowest member of your party. Don't split up. Carry a topographic map and use it often. Also, be sure to carry a compass and know how to use it. A flashlight with spare batteries can be a big help, especially if you get caught out after dark or have to spend the night in the woods.

BE BEAR AWARE

The first step of any hike in bear country is an attitude adjustment. Nothing guarantees total safety. Hiking in bear country adds a small additional risk to your trip. However, that risk can be greatly minimized by adhering to this age-old piece of advice—be prepared. And being prepared doesn't only mean having the right equipment. It also means having the right information and the right attitude. Knowledge is your best defense.

Hiking in bear country
Nobody likes surprises, and bears dislike them, too. The majority of human/ bear conflicts occur when a hiker surprises a bear. Therefore, it's vital to do everything possible to avoid these surprise meetings. Perhaps the best way is to know the five-part system. If you follow these five rules, the chance of encountering a bear on the trail sinks to the slimmest possible margin.

- Be alert.
- Don't hike alone.
- Stay on the trail.
- Don't hike in the late evening or early morning.
- Make lots of noise.

If you see a bear on the trail: Freeze and begin to slowly back away. Let the bear know you are there by clapping or talking to it in a loud voice. The bear will usually take action to avoid you. Never run from a bear, since they might consider you prey.

Cute, cuddly, and lethal: If you see a bear cub, don't go one inch closer to it. Back up and go around, or take another route, if possible. The cub might seem abandoned, but it most likely is not. Mother bear is probably very close, and female bears fiercely defend their young.

Camping In Bear Country
Using the correct bear country camping techniques can save you and the bears much grief. Once a bear has tasted human food, it often becomes habituated to this food source and many end up being destroyed. Remember, "A fed bear is a dead bear."

Staying overnight in bear country is not necessarily dangerous, but it adds a slight additional risk to your trip. The main difference is the presence of more food, cooking, and garbage. Plus, you are in bear country at night when bears are usually most active. But following a few basic rules greatly minimizes the risk to yourself and the bears.

Storing food and garbage: If your campsite doesn't have a permanent wire, pole, or locker in which to store food, be sure to hang your food well before dark. It's not only difficult to store food after darkness falls, but it's easier to miss a juicy morsel on the ground.

Find a good tree branch at least 10 feet high, hanging food at least 4 feet from the trunk. Above treeline, hang food off cliffs and boulders. Be sure to store food in airtight, waterproof bags to contain food odors. For double protection, put food and garbage in zip-locked bags and seal everything in a larger, plastic bag.

You'll need the following items to properly store and hang your food:

- A good supply of zip-locked bags.
- A waterproof "dry" bag or stuff sack for storing food.
- 75 feet of strong nylon cord.

The classic method for hanging food is tying a rock or piece of wood to the end of a rope, tossing it over a branch, and then attaching the rope to your food storage bag and hoisting it up 10 feet or more (see illustrations). Of course, don't let the rock or wood come down on your head (it happens!). Also, don't let anybody stand under the bag until you're sure it's securely in place.

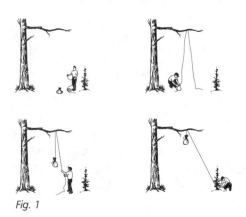

Fig. 1

Fig. 1. Hanging food and garbage over a tree branch.

Fig. 2. Hanging food and garbage over a leaning tree.

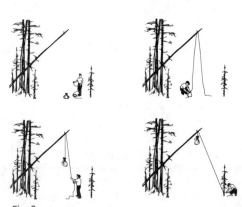

Fig. 2

What to hang: To be as safe as possible, store everything that has any food smell. This includes cooking gear, eating utensils, bags used to keep food in your pack, all garbage (stored in zip-locked bags), and even clothes with food smell on them.

Your tent (an odor-free zone): You can't be too careful in keeping food smells out of your tent. Just in case a bear has become accustomed to coming into that campsite looking for food, it's *critical* to keep all food smells out of the tent. This includes your pack, which is hard to keep odor-free, toothpaste, chapstick, lotions, and other odoriferous, non-food items.

How to cook: The overriding philosophy of cooking in bear country is to create as little odor as possible. Keep it simple. Use as few pans and dishes as possible. Unless it's a weather emergency, *never* cook in your tent.

Be careful not to spill on your clothes while cooking and eating. If you do, wash them as soon as possible and change into clean ones. Avoid leftovers by not cooking too much food and cleaning your plate to eliminate food scraps. Don't bury food or dump leftovers into any water source. Take your scrap-free dishwater at least 100 yards downwind and downhill from camp and pour it on the ground or in a small hole. Do dishes immediately after eating to minimize food smells.

Choosing a tent site: Cook and sleep at least 100 yards apart. If possible, pitch your tent *upwind* from the cooking area. Store or hang your food in the cooking area or, better yet, another 100 yards downwind of both the cooking and sleeping areas.

If you see a bear in camp or on the trail, report it to a ranger after your trip. If rangers get enough reports to spot a pattern, they manage the area to prevent potentially hazardous situations.

Spotted Lake at sunrise.

Most of the information in this section comes from *Bear Aware*, a handy, inexpensive guidebook by Falcon Publishing. The book contains even more detailed information you need to reduce the risk of having a close encounter of the bear kind. You can get this book at your local bookseller, or by calling Falcon at 1-800-582-2665.

BE MOUNTAIN LION ALERT

The most important safety element for recreation in mountain lion country is simply recognizing their habitat. Mountain lions primarily feed on deer, so these common ungulates are a key element in cougar habitat. Fish and wildlife agencies usually have good information about deer distribution from population surveys and hunting results. Basically, where you have a high deer population, you can expect to find mountain lions.

Deer tracks can be found easily on dirt roads and trails. If you are not familiar with identifying deer tracks, seek the advice of someone knowledgeable, or refer to a book on animal tracks such as Falcon's *Scats and Tracks* series.

Safety guidelines for traveling in mountain lion country

To stay as safe as possible when hiking in mountain lion country, follow this advice:

1. Travel with a friend or group. There's safety in numbers, so stay together.
2. Don't let small children wander away by themselves.
3. Don't let pets run unleashed.
4. Avoid hiking at dawn and dusk—the times mountain lions are most active.
5. Watch for warning signs of mountain lion activity.
6. Know how to behave if you encounter a mountain lion.

What to do if you encounter a mountain lion

In the vast majority of mountain lion encounters, these animals exhibit avoidance, indifference, or curiosity that seldom results in human injury. But it is natural to be alarmed if you have an encounter of any kind. Try to keep your cool and consider the following:

Recognize threatening mountain lion behavior. There are a few cues that may help you gauge the risk of attack. If a mountain lion is more than 50 yards away, and it directs its attention to you, it may be only curious. This situation represents only a slight risk to adults, but a more serious risk to unaccompanied children. At this point, you should move away, while keeping the animal in your peripheral vision. Also, look for rocks, sticks, or something to use as a weapon, just in case.

If a mountain lion is less than 50 yards away, crouched, and staring intensely at you, it may be assessing the chances of a successful attack. If this behavior continues, the risk of attack may be high.

Do not approach a mountain lion. Instead, give the animal the opportunity to move on. Slowly back away, but maintain eye contact if close. Mountain lions are not known to attack humans to defend young or a kill, but they have been reported to "charge" in rare instances to protect their territory. It's best to choose another route or time to hike through the area.

Do not run from a mountain lion. Running may stimulate a predatory response.

Make noise. If you encounter a mountain lion, be vocal and talk or yell loudly and regularly. Try not to panic. Shout in a way that makes others in the area aware of the situation.

Maintain eye contact. Eye contact presents a challenge to the mountain lion, showing you are aware of its presence. Continued eye contact also helps you keep track of where it is. However, if the behavior of the mountain lion is not threatening (if it is, for example, grooming or periodically looking away), maintain visual contact through your peripheral vision and move away.

Appear larger than you are. Raise your arms above your head and make steady waving motions. Raise your jacket or another object above your head. Do not bend over, as this will make you appear smaller and more "prey-like."

Grab the kids. If you are with small children, pick them up. First, bring children close to you, maintaining eye contact with the mountain lion, and pull the children up without bending over. If you are with other children or adults, band together.

Defend yourself. If attacked, fight back. Try to remain standing. Do not feign death. Pick up a branch or rock; pull out a knife, pepper spray, or other deterrent device. Remember that everything is a potential weapon, and individuals have fended off mountain lions with blows from rocks, tree limbs, and even cameras.

Defend others. Also, defend your hiking partners, but don't defend your pet. In past attacks on children, adults have successfully stopped attacks. However, such cases are very dangerous and risky, and physically defending a pet is not recommended.

Respect any warning signs posted by agencies.

Spread the word. Before leaving on your hike, discuss lions and teach others in your group how to behave in case of a mountain lion encounter.

Report encounters. If you have an encounter with a mountain lion, record your location and the details of the encounter, and notify the nearest landowner or land management agency. The land management agency (federal, state, or county) may want to visit the site and, if appropriate, post education/warning signs. Fish and wildlife agencies should also be notified because they record and track such encounters.

If physical injury occurs, it is important to leave the area and not disturb the site of attack. Mountain lions that have attacked people must be killed, and an undisturbed site is critical for effectively locating the dangerous mountain lion.

See Falcon Publishing's *Mountain Lion Alert* for more details and tips for safe outdoor recreation in mountain lion country.

MORE BACKCOUNTRY ESSENTIALS AND SAFETY TIPS

Wild animals can be frightening, but they're not the number-one killer of outdoor recreationists. Hypothermia is. This dangerous condition is caused when your core body temperature falls below normal. Caused by exposure and cold, it is aggravated by wind, exhaustion, and wetness. When your metabolism slows too much, less blood reaches the brain. Hypothermia deprives you of your judgment; you will not be aware of what is happening. You will lose control of your hands. You may have vicious fits of shivering, slow or slurred speech, frequent stumbling, drowsiness, exhaustion, and memory lapses. In extreme cases, it can be fatal.

The first step to preventing hypothermia is to dress in layers, in materials that can breathe. Choose rain clothes that cover you from your head to your ankles, offering good protection from the elements. The second step is fast, efficient treatment of symptoms; discuss what to do in case of hypothermia before you set out. If you observe someone with even mild symptoms, get him or her out of the wind and rain, remove all wet clothes, and administer warm drinks. Dress the victim in dry clothes if possible, and get her/him into a dry sleeping bag. A platypus or other foldable, plastic container filled with boiling water will help immensely. If the victim is suffering severely, try to keep her/him awake in a sleeping bag with another person, both stripped naked. If you have bags that zip together, and a third person is available, the victim should be placed between two warm, naked people.

By now, most backcountry visitors have heard about the protozoan *Giardia lamblia*. It won't kill you, but in some cases you may wish it had. Symptoms include severe abdominal cramps, gas and bloating, loss of appetite, and acute diarrhea. Fortunately, not all water is contaminated, but you can't tell by looking. No matter how pure the water looks, never drink from any spring, stream, river, or lake without treating the water first. It's better to be safe than sick.

There are several methods for treating water. First, you can boil all water—a good method if you want hot drinks or a boiled dinner, but a lousy idea if you need a cool drink right away. Boiling for a minimum of 1 minute at altitudes below 4,000 feet should suffice. Add several minutes of boiling time for higher altitudes; experts recommend a minimum of 5 minutes anywhere in Colorado, due to high elevation. Increase time for very high elevations or whenever the water is cloudy or muddy. Some hikers find a water purifier more convenient. Run water through the purifier and it's ready to drink. In emergencies, commercial water purification chemicals will do.

Altitude or mountain sickness is a real problem for some hikers, especially those flying in from sea level. It usually just takes two to three days to acclimate to the high altitude. If you or someone in your party feels a bit nauseated, dizzy, or has a headache and/or loss of appetite, you'll need to stop and rest. Have the victim drink water, and make sure she/he is getting plenty of sodium and high energy foods. If symptoms don't go away in a matter of time, the only option is to descend to a lower elevation where there is more oxygen.

Rocky Mountain Elk, bull (Cervus elaphus).

Take extra precautions when dealing with stormy skies. According to the National Oceanic and Atmospheric Administration (NOAA), about three hundred people in the United States die each year from lightning strikes. Many more are injured, some permanently. To avoid being struck by a lightning bolt, watch the weather. Spring and summer are the busiest seasons for lightning, though discharges can occur any time of year, even during snowstorms. Most lightning storms occur in mid- to late afternoon. Storms are usually preceded by wind and the approach of dark, towering clouds. Lightning may travel far ahead of the storm.

Seek shelter away from open ground or exposed ridges. Dropping even a few yards off a ridgetop will reduce your risk. In the forest, stay away from single, tall trees. On open ground, find a low spot free of standing water. Stay out of shallow caves, crevasses, or overhangs. During a lightning storm, assume a low crouch with only your feet touching the ground. Put a sleeping pad or pack (be sure it has no frame or other metal in it) beneath your feet for added insulation against shock. Do not huddle together; members of a group should stay at least 30 feet apart. That way, if someone is hit, the others can give CPR and first aid for burns and shock.

In a tent, get in the crouch position. Stay in your sleeping bag and keep your feet on a sleeping pad. Signs of an imminent lightning strike include hair standing on end; an itchy feeling—one hiker described it as "bugs crawling all over"—on your skin; an acrid, "hot metal" smell; and buzzing or crackling noises in the air. Tuck into a crouch immediately if any of these signs are present.

Crossing a bridgeless stream or river may be your biggest challenge in the Weminuche. Always consider depth, strength of current, width, water temperature, and clarity before you decide how, where, and when to cross. In general, cross only where the water is no more than waist-deep on the shortest member of your group. Look for shallow spots where the stream widens, at the heads and tails of islands, and on the insides of bends. Watch for strong currents. Well-developed waves or rushing vees of water indicate fast, powerful flows that can knock you down. If the current seems too fast as you wade in, retreat—it is almost always faster midstream.

Weminuche waters can be downright icy. Reduce the risk of hypothermia by keeping wading time to a minimum. For better traction and to protect your feet, wear wading shoes or Tevas or remove your socks and put your boots back on. Loosen packstraps and unhook the waistbelt so the pack can be shrugged off if you fall. A wet pack can anchor even the strongest adult to the bottom.

Cross facing sideways to the current, hips angled slightly toward the shore. Don't face downstream. Walk diagonally across the current, following a riffle or shallow bar and angling downstream if possible. Take one step at a time and test the footing before committing all your weight to it. Keep one foot secure before lifting the other. Shuffle across, always leading with the upstream leg; avoid crossing your legs. Use a hiking staff or a big stick, and hold it on your upstream side to aid in balancing. Two or more people can cross together, interlocking forearms, with the strongest person on the upstream side.

Whatever you do, don't rush across, risking a fall. You can always rest after crossing with a hot drink and some food. If you do lose your footing and are carried downstream, slide out of your packstraps and try to float downstream feet first in an upright, sitting position. Use your feet to fend off rocks or logs, and swim across the current toward shore. Carry a change of clothes in a waterproof bag, just in case.

Remember that the volume of a river can change dramatically over just a few hours. Glacier-fed streams tend to be low in the morning, then swell as afternoon heat melts ice and snow. An easy, knee-deep ford in the morning may be chest-deep and surging with power by late afternoon. Plan your return routes and crossing times carefully. All notable creek and river crossings are mentioned in this guide, with special notes on potentially dangerous fords.

Other trail dangers are smaller. Ticks are harmless, but the diseases they carry can be deadly—including Lyme disease, Colorado tick fever, and Rocky Mountain spotted fever. After traveling in tick country, watch for symptoms of tick-borne disease, including a high fever, arthritic-like pain in the bones and joints, or a rash. During tick season (spring and summer), stay out of tall grass or brushy areas, and inspect yourself and your clothing after each outing. Look for ticks nightly before going to bed. Carefully inspect your legs, groin, armpits, ears, and scalp.

To remove a loose tick, flick it off with a fingernail. If the tick is firmly imbedded in your skin, encourage it to back out by holding a hot, extinguished matchhead to its back. If the tick does not let go, use tweezers to pinch a small area around the tick's mouth to pull it out. (You may have to remove a tiny chunk of skin to get all of the tick.) Try not to squeeze the tick's body, since this increases the risk of infection. Clean the wound with an antiseptic.

Mosquitoes are more a nuisance than a danger. Most North American mosquitoes can transmit a form of encephalitis, however, which is potentially fatal. The best way to avoid mosquito-borne diseases is to avoid being bitten. Bug sprays with N, N-diethyl-3-methylbenzamide (DEET) seem to work best. Wear long pants, a long-sleeved shirt, ankle-high shoes, and a cap that covers your ears. Try not to camp near stagnant water or fields of damp or dewy grass.

TRAIL ETIQUETTE

The Weminuche is popular horse country, so hikers and horseback riders will undoubtedly meet on the trails. Please note: Riders have the right of way. Hikers, if you meet a horse on the trail, move to the down (lower) side of the trail and don't make any sudden movements or loud noises. In return, the last horseback rider should thank the hiker.

Uphill and downhill hikers will also encounter one another on the trail. Downhill hikers should always give the right of way to the uphill hiker, especially if the uphill hiker is carrying a full backpack. If you're going uphill and you want to give the trail to a downhill person so you can take a breather, that's okay, too.

You'll want to hike and explore the wilderness as quietly as possible because it's the best way to see the wildlife and avoid irritating other wilderness visitors. Keep pets under control at all times. If you can't control your pet, leave it at home.

SEASONS AND WEATHER

The hiking and backpacking season for the Weminuche Wilderness is limited to June, July, August, and September. Most trails are open from around the first of July through mid-September. Heavy snowfall regularly blankets the San Juan Mountains, which means you will find access restricted in June and perhaps even into July. Particularly hard winters have kept trails over 10,000 feet snowbound until the first week of July or even later.

High waters and dangerous crossings are one June obstacle; advantages to hiking early include fewer mosquitoes, fewer people, and more opportunities to see wildlife. July brings summer thunderstorms, with extended rainy periods. Mosquitoes are out in full force, and temperatures may be as high as the 80s, with lows dipping to the 30s and 40s. Wildflowers are at their finest during this month, and people come out in droves to see them. River levels drop to near normal.

Cooler weather is already evident by mid-August when the daily temperatures drop and autumn (a noticeable chill) is in the air. Erratic weather plagues this month: some years it's mild and fair, other years it's rainy and miserable. September is quiet in the Weminuche. The crowds are gone, and it's typically a month of low precipitation. You'll find frost on your tent most every morning, and maybe snow, too, but it should melt by noon. Streams are at their lowest and easiest for crossing while aspens dress in fall shades, adding color to an already colorful land.

Bow hunting for deer and elk begins as early as the last week of September. Until significant snow falls, causing animals to descend from the high country, hunting pressure is low. To be safe during bow and rifle season, wear a blaze orange cap or vest while traveling.

HIKING WITH CHILDREN

I've talked to many couples who have shared their love of backpacking, remembering a favorite peak or a stroll along a favorite stream. They enjoyed the peace and tranquility of an uncrowded wilderness lake—then they had kids. In their words, "That ended that."

It doesn't have to be that way. Today, more and more parents say hiking is a family sport. If properly prepared, parents can bring kids along for anything from a short stroll to an extended wilderness hike. Although hiking with children is different than hiking with adults, it isn't difficult (or so I'm told—my niece and nephew and my grandsons are just now old enough to hike.)

What kind of a hike can you expect with children? Be ready with extra clothing and supplies. Plan on plenty of breaks, covering the miles at an easy pace. Be prepared to hike at your kids' speed, stopping often to eat, play in streams or snow, and watch wildlife. For best results, think like your children. Keep them busy and happy. Don't demand a certain number of miles per day. Start with several day hikes before you set out on an extended hike or backpack. Some parents have a practice campout in the backyard before heading for the wilderness. Others choose a spot only a mile or so away from the car or trailhead for the first night out.

Bringing along Baby requires some special precautions. A baby's respiratory system can't adjust to major elevation changes until he or she reaches one year of age. Because most babies refuse to wear sunglasses, you can't take them through snow country or onto high, exposed ridges where sunburn is a threat. Short trips are best, since diapers and bottles must be carried in and out.

Toddlers are often the hardest to travel with. They're too big to carry, but not quite big enough to go long distances. Plan no more than 4 miles a day with children ages two to four. Fewer miles may be better. If your child wants to wear a pack, by all means let her do so. A tiny pack holding a jacket or toy will suffice—you'll undoubtedly end up carrying it later in the day. By the time children reach the ages of nine through twelve they'll be able to carry all of their own gear, including a fair share of the food.

Older children walk fast, often going on ahead to explore their new surroundings. Although you'll want to encourage this newfound freedom, persuade children to stick to the trail and tell them to wait for you at every fork, touching bases at each junction.

One noteworthy warning: Children of all ages will be unable to tolerate bugs, which tend to go for tender skin. Avoid buggy areas and buggy seasons for best results.

ZERO IMPACT

THREE FALCON PRINCIPLES OF ZERO IMPACT

- Leave with everything you brought in.
- Leave no sign of your visit.
- Leave the landscape as you found it.

Spend time in our nation's wilderness areas, national parks, and other prized areas, and you will find that we are oftentimes loving these places to death.

There is a proper way to behave in the wilderness: It's called Leave No Trace, a preventive education program taught by the USDA Forest Service. You've probably heard about it. It's all about being responsible, using low-impact methods of camping and traveling, taking nothing and leaving only footprints. The end result means you act as respectful in the wilderness as you would if you were visiting family or friends.

Though I've spent more than a decade hiking thousands of miles, oftentimes going for days without seeing any hint of man, it isn't always so. The Weminuche Wilderness is Colorado's most visited wilderness. If you and I follow certain guidelines then we can be better assured of leaving the place as it was meant to be. Please adhere to the following regulations:

• Self-registration at the trailhead is required. Permits are not yet needed in the Weminuche Wilderness, but standards continue to toughen. In years to come contact the managing agency for current information.

• Trails are open to primitive traffic only—mountain bikes, motorcycles, hang gliders, and other mechanical or motorized methods of travel are not allowed in wilderness areas. Accepted methods include hiking, horseback riding (although some trails are closed to horses), or packing in with your favorite animal, such as a horse, mule, llama, goat, or even a backpacking dog.

• Supervise your pets, if you bring them. Sam, my Samoyed who died several years ago, used to join me on all of my hikes and backpacking trips. In fact, he carried his own backpack. He was a pure joy and I miss him a lot. I know there are those who oppose dogs on the trails. They can be a problem at times, but I've observed leashed, quiet, and obedient pets, too. I've never seen a dog litter a trail with beer cans or candy wrappers. Keep your pet quiet, bury its waste and keep such matter away from water sources, and maintain control so it won't chase wildlife. With such care, your pet will add joy to every outing.

• Stay on the trail. If the path happens to be muddy, plow right through. Don't step off to the side. If you search for higher, drier ground, it only creates another trail; in some areas several parallel trails are being created. Be sure to hike single file. Trails several feet wide have been created because some people insist on walking side by side. (Note: If you're hiking off

Camp near the Pine River, south of Flint Creek.

trail, it is better to spread out to avoid creating new trails.) A big pet peeve of mine are those folks who cut across switchbacks. Stay on the regular route!

• Use a campstove for cooking. Some people love the warmth and comfort of a mesmerizing fire, but in certain places a fire doesn't work well. Use a portable stove unless there is ample firewood and no area restrictions against building a fire. Use wood sparingly. If you're at an established camp, use an existing fire ring. If you camp where no one has camped before, dig a hole in the dirt, then build a small fire without rocks. When the fire is out, douse the ashes with water and replace the earth. Be sure all fires are dead out.

• Carry out all litter. Do not bury trash; wild animals could dig it up. If you choose to burn your trash, remember that foil doesn't burn completely. Many wonder what to do about human waste and toilet paper. Use the "cat hole" method when nature calls. Keeping at least 200 feet from water, camp, and trails, dig down 6 inches (a lightweight garden trowel or stick works fine), setting the topsoil aside. After using this hole as a small outdoor privy, replace the dirt and topsoil, burying all matter. Stamp the soil and cover it with a few sticks or rocks if possible. You can bury toilet paper, burn it, or put it in plastic bags and pack it out with other trash. Women should carry out soiled sanitary pads and tampons.

• Camp at least 200 feet from any water source. Lakesides and meadows are appealing places to pitch a tent, but these places suffer serious, long-term damage very quickly. The USDA Forest Service requires that you camp at least 200 feet from any water source, including streams, springs, ponds, and lakes. If you want to camp near a lake, back off a bit and choose a private site. You can walk to the lake for swimming or fishing.

• Keep soaps and detergents away from the water. On extended hikes, bathing becomes necessary. You may have to wash your clothes as well. Please engage in both activities away from the water. You can bathe directly in the water only if you don't use soap, and if you aren't wearing any type of insect repellant. When brushing your teeth or using soap for washing, stay at least 200 feet from the water. Bury your toothpaste spittle. For quick wash-up jobs, carry hand wipes or waterless hand cleaner, available at automobile parts stores. Buy unscented varieties, since the scented stuff may attract bugs and bears.

• Horseback parties must limit the number of animals and persons. Groups are restricted to 15 total—for example, you're allowed 10 people and 5 pack animals. The best way to minimize livestock problems is to take as few animals as possible. One pack animal for every three or four people should suffice.

To prevent damage during short stops, tie horses to trees at least 8 inches in diameter. During long periods, tie horses to a high line that stretches between two sturdy trees so they can move about freely. To minimize trampling damage, tie, picket, or hobble horses only in dry areas. Pack animals must be picketed at least 200 feet from any water source. You'll also have to carry certified weed-free feed.

• Know fish and game regulations. Although many people enter the backcountry with relaxation, sightseeing, photography, or wildlife watching on their minds, some enter with hunting and fishing as top priorities. Those interested in the last two activities will want to check with the managing agency for up-to-date information on permits and the opening and closing dates for the season.

• Leave all "treasures" for others to see. This includes manmade stuff such as Native American artifacts, as well as rocks, wildflowers, and other plant life. Don't walk away with anything! Take only pictures; leave only footprints. If you do so, you'll come back with a mountain of memories in an album of photographs. More importantly, you'll leave a lasting treasure for generations to come.

HOW TO GET THERE

The Weminuche Wilderness is encircled by a loop that connects the towns of Silverton, Creede, South Fork, Pagosa Springs, Bayfield, and Durango. Access Silverton and Durango via U.S. Highway 550. Reach Bayfield, Pagosa Springs, and South Fork by means of U.S. Highway 160, and Creede via Colorado 149. Although most of these towns are small, you'll find telephones, gas stations, markets, restaurants, and room accommodations in all of them.

Several airlines service the Durango Airport, but flights are limited. Check with your local travel agent for more information. Greyhound offers bus service to Durango and Silverton, but not east to Pagosa Springs, South Fork, or Creede.

The Durango & Silverton Narrow Gauge Railroad provides service between Durango and Silverton, with access to wilderness trailheads at Elk Park and Needleton. The trains travel on a 36-inch track high above and beside the Animas River. Passengers see signs of yesterday's mining and railroad activities as they ascend the noble San Juan Mountains. Travel time from Durango to Silverton is 3 hours and 30 minutes. There's a slightly reduced cost for backpackers going to and from Elk Park and Needleton. If you need a lift from Needleton to Elk Park or vice versa, you can ride for a greatly reduced cost. You'll have to catch the train going north in the morning, and going south in the afternoon.

NATURAL AND HUMAN HISTORY

Colorado is a diverse state, with three major physiographic provinces: the Great Plains, in eastern Colorado, about two-fifths of the state; the Rocky Mountains, occupying the central and west central portions of the state; and the Colorado Plateau, making up the remaining western portion. Colorado's Rockies are composed of several ranges divided by wide, open basins or "parks" as they are sometimes called.

Though the Rocky Mountains can claim volcanic ancestry (they belong to the Pacific Belt, where 80 percent of the world's active volcanoes are found including the energetic peaks of the Cascades, the South American Andes, and the North American Aleutians), no active volcanoes remain here.

Mountain lion (Felis concolor).

Once, however, hot spots smoldered throughout the state, with the heart of all activity in the San Juan Mountains. Today, the San Juans' 10,000 square miles of peaks comprise the largest single range in the greater Rocky Mountains. Boasting thirteen peaks over 14,000 feet and countless more rising 11,000 feet into the heavens, the San Juans also embrace the Continental Divide.

The Continental Divide extends 1,700 miles through the United States from Montana to New Mexico. Not much more than a mild rise in the deserts of New Mexico and the flatlands of southern Wyoming, this legendary divide stands out in Colorado. Here it is easy to see, and easy to experience. Stand atop the Divide during a storm and you'll see raindrops destined for different rivers, different oceans. On the west side, raindrops end up in the Pacific Ocean; on the east side, they are destined for the Atlantic Ocean via the Gulf of Mexico. From the Divide you also can view the aftermath of heavy glacial activity as well. Cirques, U-shaped valleys, and horn-shaped peaks, all typical glacial features, are the result of heavy glacial activity about 10,000 years ago.

Colorado's several characteristic life zones stretch from the Upper Sonoran zone in the eastern Colorado plains to the Arctic-Alpine zone found above timberline. If you were to start your visit in the eastern half of the state, you would pass from the Upper Sonoran zone through the Transition-Upper Sonoran zone to the Canadian, Hudsonian, and eventually Arctic-Alpine life zones. Along the way you'd see everything from sand hills and cacti to ponderosa pine and juniper, plus treeless alpine tundra with sparse vegetation and abundant wildflowers.

This region offers an equally diverse selection of animal life. Visitors to the Weminuche often see Rocky Mountain elk, especially when traveling the higher trails. Mule deer, black bears, mountain lions, and bighorn sheep, Colorado's state animal, also live here. Mountain goats are perhaps the supreme creatures of high places. The low dips in Wyoming's Continental Divide kept goats north in Idaho, Montana, Canada, and Alaska until May 24, 1948, when nine mountain goats were released in Colorado's Sawatch Range by the Colorado Division of Wildlife. During the next 23 years, 51 goats were released in the state, including some in the area near the Needles in the Weminuche Wilderness. Travel through the Chicago Basin and you'll probably see them.

Moose were introduced into the area in January 1992, when 31 moose were released in the Rio Grande National Forest between Creede and Lake City. Since that time some of the moose have traveled south. A few of them have been seen in the wilderness along the Pine River, south of the Continental Divide.

Smaller mammals, such as coyotes, marmots, hares, rabbits, skunks, beavers, bobcats, badgers, weasels, porcupines, and squirrels, exist here as well. Bird life is abundant, too. Raptors include red-tailed hawks, prairie falcons, great horned owls, and many more. Other bird species are blue, sage, and sharp-tailed grouse; gray and Steller's jays; ravens; and a variety of wrens, bluebirds, woodpeckers, finches, sparrows, flycatchers, swallows, kinglets, hummingbirds, and blackbirds, to name a few.

The Weminuche Wilderness was named for the Weminuche Indians (now called the Ute Mountain Utes), who lived here for many years before Euroamerican explorers appeared on the scene. The earliest white explorers arrived in 1765, when Don Juan Maria de Rivera led an expedition into the area. A decade later, in 1776, two Franciscan priests, Escalante and Dominguez, established a trail connecting settlements in Santa Fe, New Mexico, and Monterey, California. They named many of the area's rivers and landmarks. Hunters, trappers, and explorers followed in the 1820s; miners came a bit later but found small amounts of ore and deemed mining unprofitable. In the late 1870s cattle and sheep ranchers discovered what is now wilderness and, although unfortunate, continue to use portions of the wilderness today.

The Weminuche Wilderness is one of many places designated wilderness by Congress as a result of the Wilderness Act of 1964. (Today there are 96 million acres of wilderness nationwide, with more than 3,000,000 acres gracing the state of Colorado.) When President Lyndon Johnson signed the Wilderness Act into effect on September 3, 1964, a portion of the law read that wilderness "shall be administered for the use and enjoyment of the American people in such a manner as will leave them unimpaired for future use and enjoyment as wilderness, and so as to provide for the protection of these areas [and] the preservation of their character." The Weminuche Wilderness received such federal protection in 1975.

1 Cunningham Gulch

Highlights:	Abundant wildflowers, wonderful views. Nice day hike; can be combined with Hike 2, Highland Mary Lakes Trail, and a short section of the Continental Divide Trail for a long loop.
Distance:	2.6 miles one-way.
Difficulty:	Strenuous.
Elevation gain and loss:	+1,380 feet, -0 feet.
Maps:	USGS Howardsville, Trails Illustrated Weminuche Wilderness.
Management:	Columbine Ranger District, San Juan National Forest.
Trail conditions:	Maintained trail; moderate use.

Finding the trailhead: From the junction of U.S. Highway 550 and Colorado 110 at the southwest end of Silverton, drive northeast on CO 110 (Greene Street) through Silverton. After 1 mile from the junction of US 550 and CO 110, go right (east), staying on CO 110. The road is paved for the first 2 miles, then turns to maintained gravel. After another 2.1 miles turn right (south) on San Juan County Road 4 (maps usually show this as Forest Road 589) toward Stony Pass. After an additional 1.7 miles the road forks again; keep right (south) on San Juan County Road 4A, which parallels Cunningham Creek. Drive 1.7 miles to another fork; park here if you don't have four-wheel-drive. The road to the left (south) ends at an old mine in 100 yards; the right (west) fork crosses the creek and continues to another unmarked trailhead after 0.7 mile or so. Those with four-wheel-drive may continue across the creek, keeping to the right as the road switchbacks up to the top and the unmarked trailhead.

Key points
1.7 Wilderness boundary.
2.6 Junction with the Continental Divide Trail.

The hike: Park at the Cunningham Creek crossing and climb the very steep, rocky road to the south for 0.5 mile. At this point, look for a trail off to the left (southeast) across the creek. Ford it, now hiking parallel to the creek along the east side. After 0.6 mile you will come to a fork. Cunningham Gulch Trail 502 is on the left (east) and leads to the Continental Divide. Be sure to sign in at the trail register before taking off on the lefthand fork. Note: The trail heading south is a wonderful return hike. See Hike 2, Highland Mary Lakes Trail.

Begin climbing at a steep (sometimes very steep!) grade. Occasional switchbacks help in the beginning, but they peter out. After a while, you'll just plain climb. The views are wonderful en route and give you plenty to

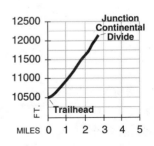

Cunningham Gulch • Highland Mary Lakes

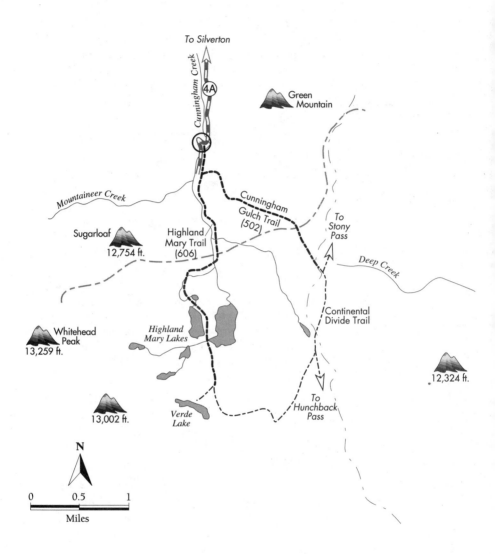

To Silverton

Cunningham Creek

4A

Green Mountain

Mountaineer Creek

Cunningham Gulch Trail (502)

To Stony Pass

Sugarloaf
12,754 ft.

Highland Mary Trail (606)

Deep Creek

Whitehead Peak
13,259 ft.

Highland Mary Lakes

Continental Divide Trail

12,324 ft.

13,002 ft.

Verde Lake

To Hunchback Pass

N

0   0.5   1
Miles

look at as you stop to catch your breath. Wildflowers are absolutely out of this world in July and August.

Enter the Weminuche Wilderness after 1.7 miles. In another 0.9 mile you'll reach the Continental Divide Trail (CDT). The CDT heads north to Stony Pass and from there goes on to Canada; it heads south to Hunchback Pass and eventually reaches Mexico.

Options: You can make a loop, long day hike, or overnight backpack by heading south on the Continental Divide Trail, then heading southwest on

23

an unmarked trail to the Highland Mary Lakes Trail (Hike 2). If you decide to do the loop (a total of 10.2 miles), you'll climb to a high point of about 12,500 feet in elevation.

To do so, check your map and head south on the Continental Divide Trail 813 (unmarked here). You'll pass two small lakes, one on the left at 0.6 mile, another on the right at 1 mile. At 1.5 miles look for a marked trail off to the right (southwest). The trail drops off from the CDT, descending into a gentle drainage before climbing at a steep grade for 50 feet or so. After 2.2 miles, the trail follows the contour line to the west, allowing for grand views and an abundance of wildflowers come summer. After 2.6 miles you'll see a trail going west to Lost Lake. Keep right, traveling north another 0.5 mile to the unmarked junction with the Highland Mary Lakes Trail.

Camping: Silverton offers a variety of private campgrounds. You can camp along the road to the trailhead, but there are no established facilities.

2 Highland Mary Lakes

See Map on Page 23

Highlights:	Abundant wildflowers, wonderful views, and high alpine tundra. Long day hike or overnight backpack. Horses not recommended. Can be combined with the Cunningham Gulch Trail and a small portion of the Continental Divide Trail for a nice loop hike (see Hike 1).
Distance:	4.5 miles one-way.
Difficulty:	Moderate to strenuous.
Elevation gain and loss:	+1,650 feet, -50 feet.
Maps:	USGS Howardsville and Storm King Peak; Trails Illustrated Weminuche Wilderness.
Management:	Columbine Ranger District, San Juan National Forest.
Trail conditions:	Maintained trail; heavy use.

Finding the trailhead: From the junction of U.S. Highway 550 and Colorado 110 at the southwest end of Silverton, drive northeast through town on CO 110 (Greene Street). After 1 mile from the junction of US 550 and CO 110, go right (east), staying on CO 110. The road is paved for the first 2 miles, then turns to maintained gravel. After another 2.1 miles turn right (south) on San Juan County Road 4 (maps usually show this as Forest Road 589) toward Stony Pass. After an additional 1.7 miles the road forks again; keep right (south) on the lower road, San Juan County Road 4A, which parallels Cunningham Creek. Drive 1.7 miles to another fork; park here if you don't have four-wheel-drive. The

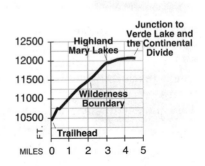

road to the left (south) ends at an old mine in 100 yards; the right (west) fork crosses the creek and continues to another unmarked trailhead after 0.7 mile. Those with four-wheel-drive may continue across the creek, keeping to the right as the road switchbacks to the top and the unmarked trailhead.

Key points
- 2.1 Wilderness boundary.
- 3.0 First of seven Highland Mary Lakes.
- 4.5 Junction with the trail to Verde Lakes and the Continental Divide Trail.

The hike: Park at the Cunningham Creek crossing and climb the very steep, rocky road to the south. After 0.5 mile, look for a trail heading off to the left (southeast) across the creek. Ford the creek and hike parallel to it, along its east side. After 0.6 mile you will come to a fork. The Cunningham Gulch Trail (Hike 1) goes left (east) here; it leads to the Continental Divide Trail and makes a wonderful trail to return on. You will pass a trail register here as you take the righthand fork.

The Highland Mary Lakes Trail 606 register appears after another 0.1 mile. Sign in here. (If you drove across Cunningham Creek and continued up the road, you'll park across the creek near here.)

From the register, the trail climbs steeply again as you wind through the trees, gaining nice views of the creek along the way. After 1.1 miles you will cross a stream. In another mile you will enter the Weminuche Wilderness. Just beyond the wilderness boundary, the main trail looks as if it continues south, but it doesn't. The wide trail just peters out. When you reach the

Wildflowers at Highland Mary Lakes.

point where Cunningham Creek meets another, unnamed creek, cross this second creek to the west and follow the maintained trail. Tree blazes mark the way.

Soon you'll be hiking out in the open. After 2.5 miles the trail descends slightly and crosses a creek. It then climbs, sometimes at a steep grade, and heads south. At 2.9 miles the route once again looks as if it will head west. It doesn't. Instead, it follows rock cairns south and up the creek. At 3 miles, cross to the east side of the creek and reach the first of seven Highland Mary Lakes (elevation 12,000 feet).

Unmaintained trails lead to the various lakes. It's easy to get around here; the high alpine tundra is open, with endless opportunities for wonderful views. The official trail passes between the two biggest lakes, continuing in a southerly direction. After reaching the easternmost lake the trail tends to fade. Keep going south from this point, following rock cairns and downed post-markers south. A wonderful view of the Grenadier Range will keep you occupied as you continue.

At 4.5 miles you'll reach a saddle and post-marker. You'll see a trail marker off to the right (west). This route leads to Verde Lake, which is visible from where you stand. Follow the trail (and post-markers) off to the left (southeast) if you want to combine this loop with the Continental Divide Trail and the Cunningham Gulch Trail. See options, below, for more details.

Options: You can combine the Highland Mary Lakes Trail with portions of the Continental Divide Trail and the Cunningham Gulch Trail (Hike 1) for a wonderful loop hike. If you decide to do the loop, a total of 10.2 miles, you'll climb to about 12,500 feet above sea level.

To make the circuit, head left (east) from the last junction mentioned in the hike description above and go upward for 0.5 mile. A trail going west to Lost Lake merges with your route here. Continue east, crossing a sideslope filled with wildflowers and good views. After 0.9 mile you'll drop a steep 50 feet to a drainage. Climb up the drainage gradually, crossing a creek at 1.1 miles. You'll meet the unsigned Continental Divide Trail 813 at 1.6 miles. Watch for rock cairns off to the south (where the CDT is en route to Hunchback Pass and eventually Mexico) and a two-track trail heading north toward Stony Pass and Canada.

Hike to the north. You'll pass a small lake at 2.1 miles and another lake at 2.5 miles as you continue to climb. After 3.1 miles keep a sharp eye out for the place where the Continental Divide Trail takes off to the northeast. The more obvious, though unsigned, trail is the Cunningham Gulch Trail (Hike 1), which heads northwest for 0.2 mile, crosses a stream, climbs a bit, then descends to Cunningham Creek.

Camping: Silverton offers a variety of private campgrounds. You can camp along the road to the trailhead, but there are no established facilities.

3 Molas Trail

Highlights:	Great views of wonderful scenes. A splendid day hike, this trail leads down into Animas Canyon and eventually to Elk Park. It's an alternative route for those who do not wish to pay for narrow-gauge train access to the Weminuche Wilderness (see Hike 5).
Distance:	4 miles one-way.
Difficulty:	Moderate.
Elevation gain and loss:	+40 feet, -1,710 feet.
Maps:	USGS Snowdon Peak, Trails Illustrated Weminuche Wilderness.
Management:	Columbine Ranger District, San Juan National Forest.
Trail conditions:	Maintained trail, heavily used. Unlike most trails in the Weminuche, this trail descends for 4 miles, making the return leg the most difficult part of the trip. Give yourself plenty of time to hike back up the switchbacks, and be sure to fill your water bottles at the river.

Finding the trailhead: From the junction of U.S. Highways 160 and 550 in south Durango, drive north on US 550 for about 43 miles. Or, drive 5.2 miles south of the quaint town of Silverton. The trailhead is about 1 mile north of Molas Pass.

Make a right (south) on the dirt road leading to the trailhead in a hundred yards or so. You'll find room to park, but nothing in the way of other amenities.

Key points
0.2   Trail register; junction with the Colorado Trail.
3.9   Elk Park Trail junction.

The hike: A trailhead sign points the way to the 469-mile Colorado Trail, which utilizes various paths in its trek from Durango to Denver. Reach the trail register at 0.2 mile. After signing in, you'll hike over easy, open terrain with wonderful views southeast to the Grenadier Range, with its spiraling faces of hardened quartzite.

You'll drop moderately for a short distance, then continue across wide meadows, climbing a tiny bit before entering the trees at 1.2 miles. Soon afterward, you'll begin dropping moderately through spruce, fir, and aspens. You'll hear Molas Creek raging off to the side. You can see Animas Canyon through the trees as you descend.

Thirty-five switchbacks (give or take one or two) make the 1,710-foot descent a pleasure. You'll finally get a glimpse of Molas Creek at

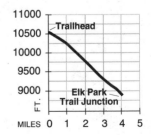

Molas Trail

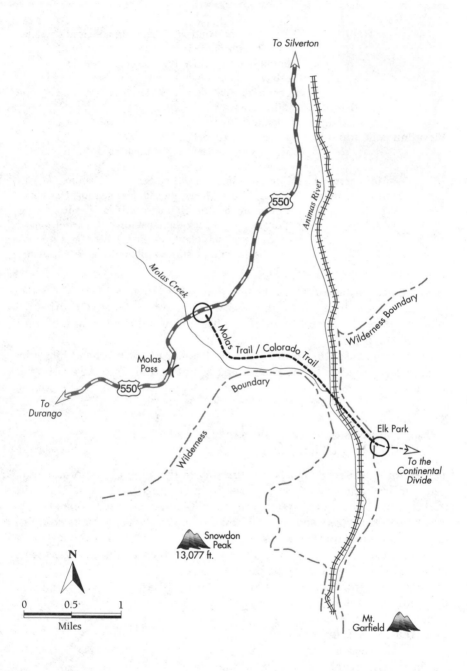

To Silverton

550

Animas River

Molas Creek

Molas Trail / Colorado Trail

Wilderness Boundary

Molas
Pass

550

Boundary

To
Durango

Elk Park

To the
Continental
Divide

Wilderness

Snowdon
Peak
13,077 ft.

N

0   0.5   1
Miles

Mt.
Garfield

Animas River at Elk Park.

2.6 miles. At the 3.6-mile point you'll cross the creek via a wooden bridge. Look for Colorado columbines, monkshood, paintbrush, and other wildflowers in this area.

Cross the Animas River via a bridge at 3.7 miles, then continue on the path. At 3.9 miles you'll follow the railroad tracks for a hundred yards or so before crossing them to reach this route's junction with the Elk Creek Trail (Hike 5).

Options: Hike this trail in midmorning or midafternoon and you may see and hear one of the Durango & Silverton Narrow Gauge trains hauling passengers between the former mining towns. The train drops off and picks up backpackers at Elk Park and further south at Needleton. (See Hike 5 and this book's introduction, under "How to get there" for further details.)

Camping: Molas Lake Park, 0.5 mile northeast of the trailhead off US 550, is an established campsite. It's a fee area; amenities include cabins in addition to campsites, showers, restrooms, and water.

4 Crater Lake

Highlights: Wildflowers, a scenic lake, and mountain views. This is a beautiful day hike or nice overnight stay.

Distance: 5.3 miles one-way.

Difficulty: Moderate.

Elevation gain and loss: +1,030 feet, -280 feet.

Maps: USGS Snowdon Peak, Trails Illustrated Weminuche Wilderness.

Management: Columbine Ranger District, San Juan National Forest.

Trail conditions: Maintained trail, heavily used.

Finding the trailhead: From the junction of U.S. Highways 160 and 550 in south Durango, drive north on US 550 for 41.9 miles. (Or, drive about 8 miles south of the quaint town of Silverton.) Make a right (south) on the paved road leading to Andrews Lake Day Use Area, driving about 0.8 mile until it ends at the lake, where there are wheelchair-accessible fishing ramps, a chemical toilet, and plenty of parking.

Key points
2.0 Wilderness boundary.
5.3 Crater Lake.

The hike: Begin by hiking up the moderate slope with a wonderful view back to Andrews Lake and beyond. You'll level off (at least for a while) after 1.2 miles. The trail next parallels a meadow, then drops some, heading through the trees, then back out into the open at 1.5 miles. Cross another meadow, then ford a creek at 1.8 miles. For the next short while, it's a moderate, sometimes steep, climb.

Enter the Weminuche Wilderness at the 2-mile point. Please note that this is a wilderness area, a place where humans are supposed to make as little impact as possible. When you pass through a wet and muddy area, don't be tempted to skirt around it. Instead of making another trail, plow right through. Use no-trace techniques to minimize your impact. (See pages 16 and 17 in introduction.)

The trail eases as you hike along the open slope laden with summer wild-flowers. The open area provides views of Hermosa Cliffs to the southwest and Engineer Mountain to the west. Descend moderately to Three Lakes Creek at 2.7 miles, one of many fords on this route. The trail stays mostly level as you cross creek after creek, alternating between trees, meadows, and open slopes. You will reach scenic Crater Lake at 5.3 miles.

Options: This is a good spot from which to climb North Twilight Peak, a jagged peak in the West Needle Mountains. The peak

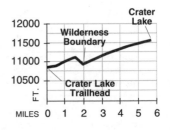

Crater Lake

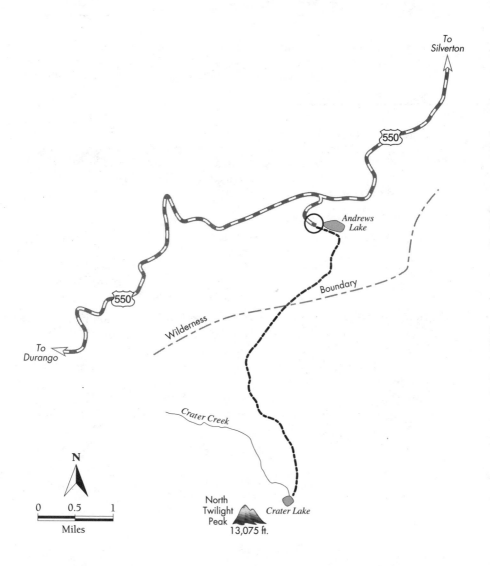

To
Silverton

550

Andrews
Lake

Boundary

550

Wilderness

To
Durango

Crater Creek

N

0   0.5   1

Miles

North
Twilight
Peak

Crater Lake

13,075 ft.

stretches to 13,075 feet above sea level. It's about 1.2 miles farther than the lake and another 1,435 feet up to the top of the mountain via the east ridge.

Camping: Molas Lake Park, about 2 miles northeast of the trailhead off US 550, is an established campsite. It's a fee area; amenities include cabins in addition to campsites, showers, restrooms, and water.

5 Elk Park/Chicago Basin Shuttle-Loop

Highlights:	Stunning vistas, wildlife, wildflowers, and waterfalls. This five- to six-day backpack is accessible by narrow-gauge railroad, or you can reach both the Elk Park and Needleton trailheads via trails.
Distance:	40.5-mile shuttle-loop.
Difficulty:	Strenuous.
Elevation gain and loss:	+8,483 feet, -8,923 feet.
Maps:	USGS Snowdon Peak, Storm King Peak, Columbine Pass, and Mountain View Crest; Trails Illustrated Weminuche Wilderness.
Management:	Columbine Ranger District, San Juan National Forest.
Special restrictions:	Campfires are no longer allowed in the Chicago Basin and Needle Creek drainages. Call the Columbine Ranger District to find out if there are any temporary fire bans in effect.
Trail conditions:	Maintained trails climb more than 12,000 feet on three occasions. Expect heavy use, since these are the most traveled trails in the wilderness.

Finding the trailhead: The Durango & Silverton Narrow Gauge Railroad provides transportation to trailheads at both Elk Park and Needleton. The latter is the busier of the two stops. You can purchase round-trip or one-way tickets to and from either location. Call the D & SNGRR at 1-888-872-4607 for more information.

If you'd rather skip the cost of a train ticket—or want to miss the mass exodus from the train dropoff—you can hike to and from Elk Park via the Molas Trail (Hike 3). It's also possible to hike to and from Needleton by

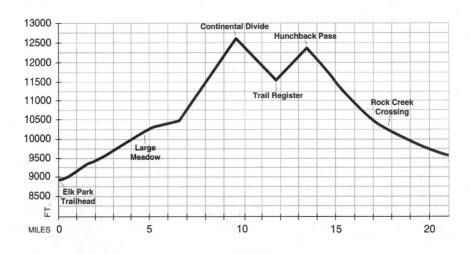

Elk Park/Chicago Basin Shuttle-Loop

using a combination of the Purgatory Creek and Animas River Trails. (See Hike 6, the Purgatory Creek/Animas River Trails, for more information.) Another option is hiking down the Molas Trail, doing the loop as described, then hopping on the train at Needleton for the short ride back to Elk Park. (Pay your fare after flagging down the engine.) From there you can hike back up to your vehicle at the Molas Trailhead.

Key points

0.3 Wilderness boundary.
4.6 Large meadow.
8.4 Old miner's cabin.
9.4 Continental Divide.
13.2 Hunchback Pass.
17.8 Rock Creek crossing.
23.3 Bridge over Vallecito Creek.
31.5 Columbine Pass.
38.0 New York Creek.
39.8 Wilderness boundary.
40.5 Needleton.

The hike: If you arrive at the Elk Creek Trailhead on foot, hike the Elk Creek Trail (part of the more extensive Colorado Trail), about 0.8 mile from the Animas River bridge where you'll meet up with the spur trail on the southeast side of the tracks leading from the train dropoff point. If you arrive by train, follow the side tracks east 100 yards or so to a trail that heads northeast. It's a steep climb to the main trail at 0.3 mile. At the point where both trails merge, head east and immediately enter the Weminuche Wilderness. There's a registration box just ahead in 100 yards or so.

The trail climbs at a moderate grade, descending on occasion. You'll pass a lovely waterfall at 0.8 mile. You can see and hear Elk Creek at various points along the way. Look for Colorado columbines, bluebells, and other wildflowers en route.

The trail steepens after 2 miles, with several switchbacks leading to a point above the river at 2.5 miles. You can catch good views here before entering the trees. At 3 and 3.1 miles you'll cross small creeks, after which you'll negotiate a short, but very steep, grade. At 3.2 miles you can see Electric Peak and Vestal Peak, striking summits of the Grenadier Range.

For the next 0.2 mile you'll climb at a moderate grade to where the trail is fairly level. At 3.6 miles you'll reach some beaver ponds. If you head southeast from here, you can make a sidetrip up to the base of Vestal, Ar-

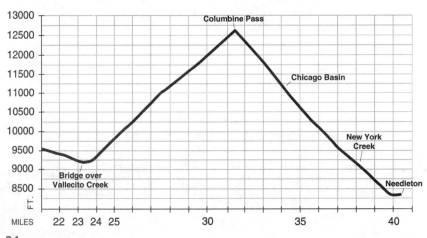

34

row, and Electric Peaks. There are excellent places to camp near these peaks, and it's a great place to climb.

On the main shuttle-loop route, you'll pass through a maze of rocks, then trees, before reaching a large, flat meadow at 4.6 miles. There you are surrounded by 13,000-foot-plus peaks. You can see west to the West Needle Mountains, north to Arrow Mountain, southeast to Peak Two, and southwest to Electric Peak. It's a sight you won't soon forget.

At the east end of the meadow you'll reenter the trees. The trail climbs at a fairly easy pace, continuing to parallel scenic Elk Creek and crossing several smaller creeks along the way. Cross a larger creek with a log bridge and hand railing at 5.7 miles. At 6.1 miles the trail steepens, passing across an occasional open sideslope with a potpourri of colorful wildflowers. After 6.7 miles the grade gets even steeper. Take plenty of time to stop, catch your breath, and enjoy the surrounding scenes as you begin to climb above treeline.

At 7.3 miles the trail eases up somewhat, but the views remain. Turn your head to the southeast and look for a double waterfall. You'll pass some large rockfalls (look for pikas) and fragile meadows. Though it may not be shown on the map, you'll cross Elk Creek at 7.8 miles; you may have to get your feet wet. You'll cross the creek again shortly thereafter. The trail is steep from this second crossing to 8.4 miles, where there's an old miner's cabin. You may want to stay here a while, enjoying the view of this lovely basin.

After you've rested, continue upward. A series of two dozen or so switchbacks begins at 8.7 miles. The moderate grade and abundant wildflowers will get you to the Continental Divide (elevation 12,650 feet) and a trail junction at 9.4 miles. Going left (north) here allows you to continue on the Colorado Trail, head north to Stony Pass, or continue on to Hunchback Pass. The south (right) trail leads to Eldorado Lake, Kite Lake, and also on to Hunchback Pass (see Hike 39).

To complete the shuttle-loop, head north. It's a gradual downhill to a fork at 9.7 miles. Keep to the right (northeast) at this junction; the lefthand (northwest) trail heads to Stony Pass. Descend the steep righthand trail, which parallels another trail leading northwest and merges with it at the 10-mile point. Reach an unsigned junction at 10.7 miles: The east (straight ahead) trail continues access on the Colorado Trail; go right (southeast) to continue this loop.

You'll exit the wilderness now, continuing the steep downhill to where you cross Bear Creek at 11.2 miles. After another 0.3 mile (at 11.5 miles) the trail ends at a four-wheel-drive road; go right (west) to continue to Hunchback Pass.

Reach a trail register and signed post pointing the way to Hunchback Pass at 11.6 miles. Turn left (south). You are now hiking the Continental Divide Trail. If you want to make a sidetrip to Kite Lake, continue up the old road for another 0.4 mile—you'll find the lake, an old miner's cabin, and a couple of mine shafts, but not much in the way of flat camping spots.

Back on the main route, you'll cross several creeks as you wind upward at a moderate to steep grade. There are lovely views of small tarns and big mountains from here. You'll see some old mine remains en route to Hunch-back Pass (elevation 12,493 feet) and the wilderness boundary at 13.2 miles. From the pass you can gaze south toward the Guardian, the most prominent peak in view, and farther south into the Needle Mountains.

Beyond the pass, the trail makes a very steep descent to the 13.5-mile point and a creek crossing. The trail then levels out some, but soon descends again as it parallels the headwaters of Vallecito Creek. Wildflowers and plant life are abundant come summer, with paintbrush, marsh marigolds, bluebells, hellebore, and other flowers in bloom.

Cross Vallecito Creek at 14.2 miles, and continue the moderate to steep descent. You'll reach the trees in another 0.3 mile. At 14.7 miles you'll reach an unsigned trail junction. At this point the Continental Divide Trail goes east to Nebo Pass. You'll continue south instead on the Vallecito Trail.

For a short distance the trail parallels Nebo Creek, a lovely creek with little cascades and small pools. After reaching the 15-mile point, you'll head back along Vallecito Creek, then cross it. Look for waterfalls, cascades, and pools as you descend the moderate (sometimes steep) slope. Cross Vallecito Creek again at 15.4 miles.

Beyond the 16-mile point, the trail follows Vallecito Creek, mostly staying in the trees but venturing out into a number of lovely meadows en route. Here you'll be blessed with not only wildflowers and aspens but also wonderful views of the surrounding high peaks. Along the way, you'll cross numerous small streams.

There are several places to camp near the Rock Creek crossing at 17.8 miles. Remember to camp at least 200 feet from any water source. Be prepared to get your feet wet at the crossing. As you continue, the trail grade stays mostly moderate. You'll find more nice places to camp as you continue.

At 20.5 miles you'll climb moderately, winding up through the trees. After another 0.7 mile you'll ford Roell Creek. There are more creek crossings before the trail heads back to Vallecito Creek and the turnoff for the bridge crossing at 23.3 miles. Make a right (west) at this turnoff and hike 100 yards or so to the bridge. After crossing the bridge, you'll hike on nearly level terrain, passing many good places to camp before and after you ford Johnson Creek at 23.8 miles.

The next section of the hike goes through pines and aspens, continuing at an easy pace until the 24-mile point. The trail then climbs at a steeper grade. You'll see Johnson Creek off and on as you continue. After 24.5 miles you must ford Grizzly Gulch. Cross another small, unnamed creek at 25.1 miles.

Over the next 0.2 mile, moderate, sometimes steep, switchbacks through the pines make life easier. Be sure to stop and observe Johnson Creek along the way; its thunderous waters plummet through wonderful rock canyons. Places to camp are limited as you climb.

The valley opens up after 26.5 miles, with good views of surrounding peaks. Moderate but sometimes steep switchbacks begin at 26.7 miles. Trees grow sparse now, and wildflowers make an appearance. You'll cross a big rock slide at 27.5 miles. Just beyond it, the switchbacks end.

Mountain goats in the Chicago Basin.

You'll have to cross several small streams as you continue, including the stream flowing from Hazel Lake at 28.5 miles. The trail steepens at 28.8 miles. Old mining relics just off the trail at the 30-mile point may interest some. Others may be more absorbed in the yellow columbines, sulphur paintbrush, and sunflower-like flowers found along the way.

At 30.9 miles the trail crosses a stream from Columbine Lake. You'll reach the lake itself in another 0.2 mile. Camping is limited at the lake, which is surrounded by very fragile terrain.

It's a very steep climb from the lake to Columbine Pass (elevation 12,680 feet) at 31.5 miles. From here you get fantastic views of countless high peaks ranging from 12,000 to more than 14,000 feet above sea level. You can see north into the Chicago Basin and as far as the Needle Mountains. Looking back southeast you'll spot the glacier-carved Johnson Creek drainage, bordered by McCauly Peak, Echo Mountain, Organ Mountain, Amherst Mountain, Mount Valois, and Florida Mountain.

A very steep downhill drops you off the north side of the pass very quickly. You are now on the Needle Creek Trail, which descends at a steep grade, with switchbacks eventually leading down into the trees. You'll come to a creek crossing at 33.2 miles. There are places to camp here above the Chicago Basin, a place less crowded than the depths of the basin below. The views are wonderful, too.

From here it's a steep descent past an old mineshaft and cabin at 33.5 miles. A few switchbacks lead into the Chicago Basin at 33.7 miles. Cross a stream at 34 miles.

Ford Needle Creek at 34.1 miles. The trail descends at an easy to moderate grade, with creek crossings at 34.6 and 34.8 miles. There are some places to camp in the trees and on the outskirts of a meadow where there are wonderful views of the Weminuche's three 14,000-footers—Mount Eolus (14,083 feet), Sunlight Peak (14,059 feet), and Windom Peak (14,082 feet).

Enter the trees at 35.6 miles and continue descending. There's another creek crossing before you reach Needle Creek, which offers a lovely water-fall at 37.5 miles. Fortunately, there's a bridge over New York Creek at 38 miles.

The trail eases up some after 38.5 miles. You'll find a combination of aspens and pines in this area. Exit the wilderness at 39.8 miles. There's a trail register at the boundary for those hiking in, and a trail junction. Go left (south) here if you're hiking to the trailhead at Purgatory Creek; it's a total of 11.6 miles from here to the trailhead. If you're returning by train, go right (north) to Needleton. It's an easy walk to the bridge over the Animas River at 40.5 miles. You'll see a posted sign noting the train stop. This is a flagged stop, so be sure to wave your hands in front of your knees to get the conductor to stop. If it's raining and you need a dry place to hang out while waiting for the train, walk downriver 200 feet or so to an abandoned cabin. The roof doesn't leak. I should know.

Options: If you're interested in hiking to Trimble Pass via the Endlich Mesa Trail, you'll pass the trail junction 60 feet or so below Columbine Pass. (See Hike 8, Endlich Mesa/Burnt Timber Shuttle-Loop for additional information.) Another great sidetrip heads up to Nebo Pass from mile 14.7. It's 1.6 miles and 930 feet up to the Continental Divide at Nebo Lake and a grand east-west view.

Camping: Purgatory Campground is a fee area with water and outhouses.

6 Purgatory Creek/Animas River Trails

Highlights:	Scenic canyons and access to the wilderness. This route provides an alternative to using the train to get to the Chicago Basin (Hike 5). It's a day hike to the Animas River and back or a two- to three-day backpack if you explore Animas Canyon.
Distance:	11.3 miles one-way.
Difficulty:	Moderate to strenuous.
Elevation gain and loss:	+900 feet, -1,500 feet.
Maps:	USGS Engineer Mountain, Electra Lake, and Mountain View Crest; Trails Illustrated Weminuche Wilderness.
Management:	Columbine Ranger District, San Juan National Forest.
Trail conditions:	Maintained trail, heavy use. Unlike most Weminuche Trails, this one first descends then climbs back to the trailhead. Allow extra time for the return leg.

Purgatory Creek/Animas River Trails

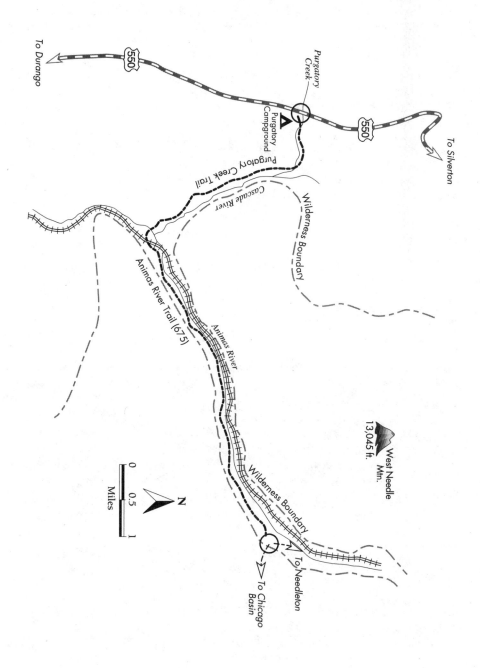

To Durango

550

Purgatory Creek

550

To Silverton

Purgatory Campground

Purgatory Creek Trail

Cascade River

Wilderness Boundary

Animas River Trail (675)

Animas River

West Needle Mtn.
13,045 ft.

Wilderness Boundary

N

0   0.5   1
Miles

To Chicago Basin

To Needleton

Finding the trailhead: From the junction of U.S. Highways 160 and 550 in south Durango, drive north on US 550 for 26.7 miles and turn right (east) on Forest Road 593. The trailhead is right off the road; Purgatory Campground is just beyond. The trailhead and campground are not well marked. If you can't find them, look for milepost 49; they're right across from Purgatory Ski Area.

Key points
2.2   Gate.
4.6   Animas River crossing.
11.3 Needle Creek Trail junction.

The hike: Walk about 100 yards from the trailhead and you'll find the trail register. After signing in follow the Purgatory Creek Trail past a mix of wild roses, cows, and cow dung. You'll hear and sometimes see Purgatory Creek off to the north. Descend through pines an aspens, switchbacking moderately. Cross Purgatory Creek at 0.6 mile.

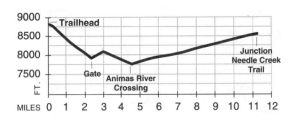

At 1.4 miles you'll cross a little stream, then hike across Purgatory Flats, which are west of the Cascade River. After 2.2 miles you'll reach a gate. Please close it after you

Durango and Silverton narrow-gauge train crossing the Animas River near Cascade Wye.

pass through, to prevent cattle from ruining the canyon and its lush vegetation. You'll see bluebells and many more wildflowers as you walk.

Climb along the narrow canyon walls, ascending to about 300 feet above the creek at times. You'll reach a nice ponderosa pine overlook at the 3-mile point. Catch good views of Cascade Canyon and a wonderful view toward Animas Canyon.

As you hike farther along the trail, look up Cascade Canyon for a view to Engineer Mountain. The canyon widens some as the trail descends through a mix of pines and aspens. There's another ponderosa-decorated overlook at 4.1 miles, with a nice view of several peaks to the north. Switchback down now, reaching a junction at 4.5 miles. Keep left at this point, heading up the Animas River. There are nice places to camp in the area.

At 4.6 miles you'll cross the Animas River via a bridge and come to a sign reading "Cascade Wye," denoting a wide spot along the river. You'll want to follow the trail upstream (northeast), crossing the narrow gauge railroad tracks at 4.8 miles. The Animas River Trail 675 runs parallel to the Animas River and slowly climbs, rising 600 feet over more than 6 miles. It takes you past ponderosa pines, Colorado columbines, wild roses, and many more lovely plants. There are nice places to camp along the way.

Take your time. You'll reach the Needle Creek Trail junction at 11.3 miles.

Camping: Purgatory Campground is a fee area with water and outhouses.

---

7 Lime Mesa

Highlights:	Wildflowers and wonderful views, including the Needle Mountains. Nice day hike in a stunning place to explore on your own.
Distance:	3.6 miles one-way.
Difficulty:	Easy to moderate.
Elevation gain and loss:	+1,000 feet, -50 feet.
Maps:	USGS Mountain View Crest; Trails Illustrated Weminuche Wilderness.
Management:	Columbine Ranger District, San Juan National Forest.
Trail conditions:	Maintained trail, light use. Sheep graze here during summer.

Finding the trailhead: From the junction of U.S. Highways 550 and 160 in south Durango, head north on US 550. After 1.4 miles make a right on 32nd Street and drive 1.3 miles until the street ends at Florida Avenue (La Plata County Road 250). Make a left (north), staying on La Plata CR 250 for 9.4 miles to Missionary Ridge Road (La Plata County Road 253). Turn and follow this well-maintained gravel road with numerous switchbacks. It becomes Forest Road 682 en route to Henderson Lake at 11.7 miles. Continue past the lake; after another 6.5 miles the road is renamed Henderson Lake

Lime Mesa

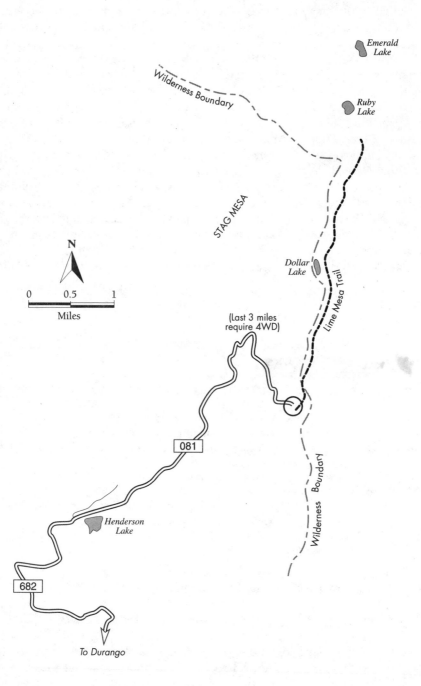

Emerald
Lake

Wilderness Boundary

Ruby
Lake

STAG MESA

Dollar
Lake

Lime Mesa Trail

N

0   0.5   1

Miles

(Last 3 miles
require 4WD)

081

Wilderness Boundary

Henderson
Lake

682

To Durango

Hikers at Dollar Lake.

Road (Forest Road 081). Drive an additional 3.1 miles and park if you are in a low-clearance vehicle. You'll need four-wheel-drive to go the remaining 2.1 miles to the trailhead.

Key points
- 0.2 Wilderness boundary.
- 1.9 Dollar Lake.

The hike: Sign the register, which you'll find at the trailhead, then begin your hike. You'll slowly gain altitude as you walk across Lime Mesa. You'll enter small stands of trees on occasion, but the nicest thing about this hike is that you stay mainly out in the open, where wonderful views are yours for the asking.

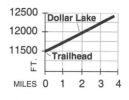

You will enter the Weminuche Wilderness after 0.2 mile. In another 0.2 mile, a sign points the way to Durango Reservoir. The Trails Illustrated map shows a trail heading east to the reservoir from here, but I couldn't find the trail junction. The country is wide open here, so you can try to find the trail if you so desire.

Our route continues straight ahead. After 1.9 miles you'll reach Dollar Lake, home to marmots and other critters. Continue on, traveling past a small tarn and numerous wildflowers (in July) until the trail ends at 3.6 miles.

From the end of the trail you'll see Ruby and Emerald Lakes below. Look north and across the Chicago Basin to Pigeon and Turret Peaks. Both are close to 14,000 feet high, certainly dramatic. In addition, you'll see numer-

43

ous other peaks forming the Needle Mountains. Three fourteeners—Mount Eolus, Sunlight Peak, and Windom Peak—make the Chicago Basin the most popular area in the wilderness.

Options: You'll see quite a few unmaintained trails in this area. Many of them are sheep trails, but some lead to various wildflower-covered knobs and peaks. The country is wide open, making cross-country travel a delight. Be sure you know how to use your map and compass.

Camping: Although Henderson Lake has no designated campground, there are places to camp en route to the lake and beyond.

8 Endlich Mesa/Burnt Timber Shuttle-Loop

Highlights:	Wildflowers, wildlife, grand views, and a scenic lake. This is a three- to four-day backpack if you arrange for a shuttle. The first few miles from either end make nice day hikes.
Distance:	23.8-mile shuttle-loop.
Difficulty:	Moderate to strenuous.
Elevation gain and loss:	+2,550 feet, -5,190 feet.
Maps:	USGS Lemon Reservoir, Vallecito Reservoir, Columbine Pass, and Mountain View Crest; Trails Illustrated Weminuche Wilderness.
Management:	Columbine Ranger District, San Juan National Forest.
Trail conditions:	Maintained trails with possible high creek crossings. Light use, but sometimes busy around City Reservoir.

Finding the trailhead: To reach the trailhead at Endlich Mesa, drive from the junction of U.S. Highways 160 and 550 (Camino Del Rio) in south Durango, traveling north on US 550. After 0.4 mile make a right (east) on East 8th Street, heading through historic downtown. Drive another 0.3 mile before bearing left (north) on East 3rd Avenue. This becomes Florida Avenue (La Plata County Road 240) upon reaching 15th Street.

After 14.7 miles you will reach a fork in the road. Head left (north) on gravel La Plata County Road 243, soon entering San Juan National Forest. Pass Miller Creek Campground after 3.1 miles and continue another 3.8 miles to the turnoff for East Florida Road 597 on the right. This long, bumpy road (passable with a high-clearance vehicle) climbs 11 miles to the start of this trail loop; it'll take about an hour to drive. The road ends at the trailhead; facilities are nonexistent.

To drop a shuttle car off at the endpoint trailhead, continue 0.2 mile to Florida Campground, traveling through the campground and keeping to the left as you continue on to Transfer Park Campground. The trailhead and

Endlich Mesa/Burnt Timber Shuttle-Loop

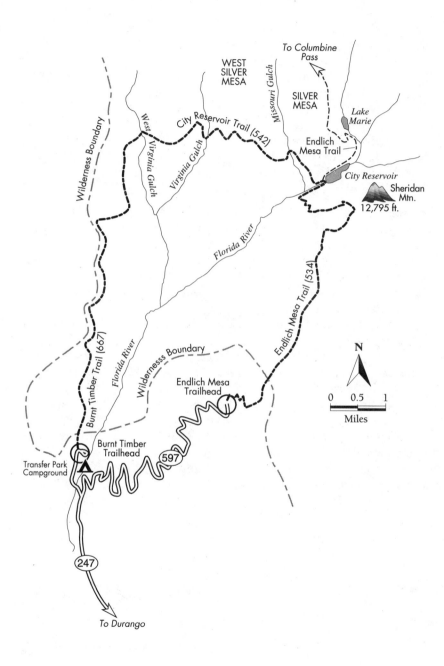

campground entrance are in another 1.3 miles. There's plenty of room for parking at the trailhead, plus room to unload horses.

Key points
- 2.0 Wilderness boundary.
- 6.0 Saddle; high point along this trail.
- 6.2 Fork; bear left.
- 8.4 Florida Creek ford.
- 9.0 City Reservoir.
- 10.3 Missouri Gulch ford.
- 12.4 High point at West Silver Mesa.
- 13.7 Virginia Gulch ford.
- 15.8 West Virginia Gulch.
- 16.8 Junction; Burnt Timber Trail and Lime Mesa Stock Trail.
- 23.4 Wilderness boundary.

The hike: Endlich Mesa Trail 534 begins at the northeast tip of the parking area atop Endlich Mesa. An old logging road serves as the trail, heading northeast through open woods. Rock cairns mark the way, freeing you to concentrate on the many species of summer wildflowers. After climbing moderately for 1.2 miles, you'll break out of the trees. The trail grade remains moderate, even gradual, as you head to the 2-mile point. You'll enter the wilderness area around this time.

The trail is a series of small roller coasters: it climbs, descends a bit, then climbs some more, traveling across alpine tundra with see-forever views. To the west you can look at Missionary Ridge (just across the Florida drainage) and, farther west, the La Plata Mountains. Look north to see a portion of the jagged Needle Mountains, and east for more of the rugged Weminuche Wilderness. Nearby, a rainbow of wildflowers grows amid granite slabs and boulders, some of which are covered with colorful lichen.

After 6 miles you'll come to a saddle at 12,110 feet above sea level; this is the high point on this trail. If no thunderstorms threaten, you can sit here and enjoy the view of 12,795-foot Sheridan Mountain to the northeast. When you're done gazing, drop into the basin, reaching a fork in 6.2 miles. Rock

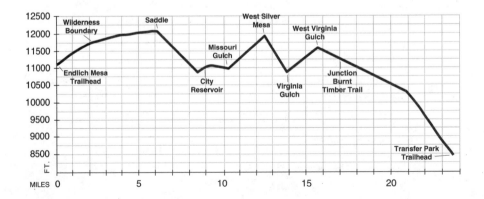

cairns mark both trails, but you'll want to head left (north), continuing to descend on the steep trail. The unmaintained trail heading straight (east), follows the contour line to another saddle and accesses a lake on the east side of the ridge.

Descend via the rerouted trail, which was created because the old trail was too steep and eroded. Stay on the new trail, descending moderate switchbacks to Florida Creek at 8.4 miles. Ford the creek, traveling east between the waters of Missouri Gulch and Florida Creek. Missouri Gulch soon disappears, but you'll continue to parallel Florida Creek, climbing a mostly steep grade to the 9-mile point and the southwest end of City Reservoir. Here you'll find City Reservoir Trail 542. Camping spots are limited at the lake, but you will find a few sites at the northeast and southwest ends; also look on the west slope for previously used sites.

From the southwest end of City Reservoir, hike west on City Reservoir Trail, making sure to use the upper trail. (If you can't see a trail below you, you're not on the upper trail and you need to be.) The trail is nearly level as you begin, but turns into a short steep uphill at 9.2 miles as you head into the trees. The trail levels off then descends gradually to a stream crossing at 9.5 miles. You'll climb steeply to 9.6 miles. Soon afterward, look for a waterfall on the left.

At 10 miles the Missouri Gulch drainage widens and the grade lessens. Here you hike through a wildflower-blessed open forest with plenty of room to camp. Rockhop across a stream at 10.2 miles. Immediately afterward, the trail forks. Head left and down into the meadow. In another 0.1 mile you'll have to ford Missouri Gulch.

Beyond the gulch, head back into the trees via a moderate to steep trail. You'll come to another fork at 10.8 miles. Rock cairns point the way to the high trail, your route. The lower trail leads to a camping area more than a mile away, used by herders in summer and hunters in the fall. The countryside gets rugged below the camps.

The high trail is sometimes very steep as you climb to the southern edge of the flower- and limestone-laden West Silver Mesa at 11.5 miles. You'll reach a 12,000-foot elevation just beyond. Begin a gradual downhill, crossing a stream at 12.8 miles. As you descend, watch and listen for elk; this is prime summer habitat for these amazing creatures. You'll cross a stream at 13.5 miles, then enter an enormous meadow where there are wildflowers and nice views to the north. There are good places to camp in the trees.

After another 0.2 mile ford Virginia Gulch, then continue across the meadow and into the trees. Pass a rock outcrop at 13.8 miles, a fun place to watch for marmots and pikas. It's a moderate climb (with some steep pitches) up to 14.4 and 14.9 miles, where you'll cross more streams. The trail tops off at 15.6 miles, then it's out into the open. You'll cross West Virginia Gulch at 15.8 miles. Explore this high mesa and you'll find several tiny ponds and places to camp in the trees at meadow's edge.

The trail stays nearly level as you hike to a fork in the trail at 16.8 miles. A sign points west to "Lime Mesa Stock Trail – 1/2 mile"; it's straight ahead to "Transfer Park – 7 miles." Stay straight. You are now hiking Burnt Timber

Virginia Gulch at sunset.

Trail 667. As you continue along the ridge, moderately descending, you'll get nice views to the east including Sheridan Mountain, Endlich Mesa, and other points.

At 17.4 miles the trail turns and heads west. It then turns southeast at 18.4 miles, later heading south as you choose one of many trails in the area. Please do not add to the problem by making another trail. The route stays fairly level across the west edge of a previously logged meadow. The wilderness has never been logged—the trail just meanders inside and outside of its western boundary.

At 19.3 miles you'll find yourself walking on an open road. You'll cross a creek soon after, then come to a fork at 19.6 miles. Leave the road here, taking the lefthand trail through the woods and out into a vast meadow and slope where there are numerous wildflowers in midsummer, as well as lodgepole pine and some fir. Continue to descend to 20.8 miles.

The trail levels off for a while. Enjoy it while you can. Near the 21-mile mark you'll begin descending again. At first it's a moderate drop, but it then becomes a very steep grade. You'll cross several creeks en route, including New Burnt Timber, Burnt Timber, and South Burnt Timber Creeks. Notice the lovely groves of aspen that pop up about this time.

The trail grade eases at times, allowing you to enjoy the aspen, the variety of wildflowers, and the numerous other plants and trees, including scrub oak and ponderosa pine in the lower realms. You'll exit the wilderness at 23.4 miles. The Transfer Park Trailhead and end of the partial loop follow at 23.8 miles.

Options: If you do nothing else while you camp near City Reservoir, be sure to explore the Florida Creek drainage. Its quiet pools, raging waterfalls, tumbling cascades, amazing slabs of granite, and abundant wildflowers—columbine, hellebore, bistort, bluebells, paintbrush, and elephants head, to name a few—combine to make this a stunning place.

The Endlich Mesa Trail does not end at City Reservoir. You can continue on to the upper end of City Reservoir at 0.7 mile, then climb a steep grade to Lake Marie at 1.6 miles. From there, continue up a very steep ridge to the west, reaching its crest at 1.8 miles. After 2.4 miles the trail gradually climbs the alpine tundra of Silver Mesa. Here, tiny ponds mirror granite slabs and boulders decorated with lichen and phlox. At 2.7 miles you'll reach the edge of a ridge overlooking Lake Marie and the Florida drainage, also known as Crystal Valley. You can continue another 4 miles or so across this wide open mesa, traveling over Trimble Pass (elevation 12,860 feet) to trail's end at 12,680-foot Columbine Pass.

Camping: Florida Campground, located near the trailhead, is a fee area with drinking water. Transfer Park Campground, at trail's end, is also a fee area with drinking water.

9 Vallecito Creek Trail

Highlights:	Wildflowers, and a lovely creek with tiny pools and waterfalls. A stunning day hike on the first few miles of trail, or a wonderful four- to five-day backpack trip.
Distance:	19.5 miles one-way.
Difficulty:	Easy to moderate; strenuous farther up.
Elevation gain and loss:	+4,793 feet, -300 feet.
Maps:	USGS Vallecito Reservoir, Columbine Pass, and Storm King Peak; Trails Illustrated Weminuche Wilderness.
Management:	Columbine Ranger District, San Juan National Forest.
Trail conditions:	Maintained trail with heavy traffic, especially on weekends and holidays.

Finding the trailhead: About 18 miles east of Durango via U.S. Highway 160, you'll find the small town of Bayfield. From there, head north on paved Vallecito Lake Road (La Plata County Road 501). After 8.9 miles you'll reach a junction with La Plata County Road 240, another possible route if you're coming from Durango. Keep straight (north) on CR 501.

After an additional 9.9 miles you'll come to another fork. Bear left (north) here on paved La Plata County Road 500 to reach the Vallecito Campground and trailhead parking in 2.8 miles. There's a picnic area and outhouse at the trailhead, plus plenty of room for both automobiles and horse trailer parking.

Key points
- 0.6   Wilderness boundary.
- 3.4   Taylor Creek ford; bridge across Vallecito Creek.
- 5.6   Second Creek ford.
- 7.1   Hanging bridge over Vallecito Creek.
- 9.3   Bridge over Vallecito Creek; access to Johnson Creek.

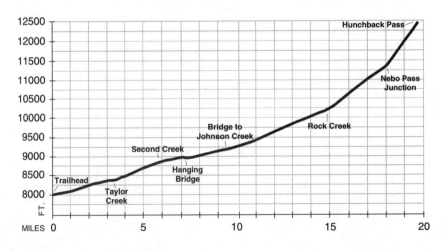

Vallecito Creek Trail

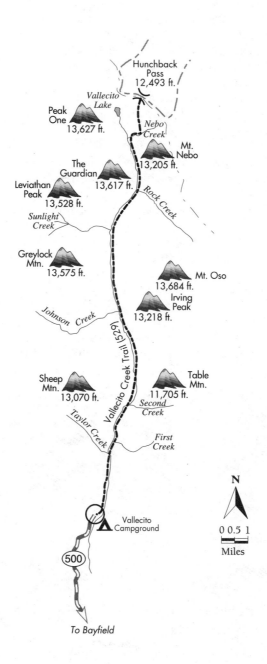

Hunchback
Pass
12,493 ft.

Vallecito Lake

Peak
One
13,627 ft.

Nebo Creek

Mt.
Nebo
13,205 ft.

The
Guardian
13,617 ft.

Leviathan
Peak
13,528 ft.

Rock Creek

Sunlight Creek

Greylock
Mtn.
13,575 ft.

Mt. Oso
13,684 ft.

Irving
Peak
13,218 ft.

Johnson Creek

Vallecito Creek Trail (529)

Sheep
Mtn.
13,070 ft.

Table
Mtn.
11,705 ft.

Second Creek

Taylor Creek

First Creek

Vallecito
Campground

N

0 0.5 1
Miles

500

To Bayfield

14.8 Rock Creek ford.

17.9 Unsigned junction to Nebo Pass.

19.4 Hunchback Pass.

The hike: Vallecito Creek Trail 529 begins in a ponderosa pine forest interspersed with aspens and conifers amid the steep granite walls of a narrow, impressive canyon. The trail skirts the western edge of the Vallecito Campground, reaching the north end in 0.5 mile. Soon afterward you will cross Fall Creek via a bridge.

The trail then climbs gradually, entering the wilderness after 0.6 mile. The route then splits for 0.5 mile or so: horseback riders bear left, while hikers continue straight ahead. At the 1-mile mark you'll head away from the steep canyon walls, climbing the ridge between the Vallecito Creek drainage to the east and the Weasel Skin and Fall Creek drainages to the west. Around 1.2 miles you'll come out onto a semi-open slope of granite and various trees.

The trail climbs gradually, gently descending now and then as you parallel the creek. You'll start out high above the water, then descend and hike next to it. Along the way there are wildflowers. Look for fireweed, daisies, blue columbines, wild geraniums, and a whole lot more.

The trail splits again at 1.7 miles, this time for only 0.1 mile: hikers head right, horses bear left. In a short distance you'll see up the drainage to the pointed crown of Irving Peak. Switchback down and meet the river up close and personal at 2 miles.

After 3.4 miles you'll have to ford Taylor Creek. Later in the season it's possible to rockhop, but before that you may have to get your feet wet. Just

Waterfalls along Vallecito Creek.

after crossing, you'll find a place to camp in an aspen grove. This area gets a lot of use, so please continue on if you can.

You'll cross Vallecito Creek at this point. Fortunately, a bridge makes for an easy crossing. If you need a place to camp, look for a spur trail taking off to the right as you continue north along the east side of the creek. Proceed up the trail if you can, fording First Creek at 3.9 miles. The gradual to moderate climb continues across a slope, then heads back along Vallecito Creek in a mile or so. There's a grove of aspens on a bench above the river at 5.1 miles. You may find a nice place to camp in this area.

Ford Second Creek at 5.6 miles. You'll cross another bridge soon after, now traveling along the west side of the creek. Pass by some campsites that are close to the water as you continue. You'll see a huge variety of wildflowers here come summer. On an open slope you may spot wild roses, some sort of orange lily, columbines, geraniums, violets, wild chives, daisies, bluebells, and wild strawberries, to name a few.

The trail crosses a side creek at 6.9 miles, then goes across another bridge—this one a hanging bridge—over Vallecito Creek at 7.1 miles. From here there's an even better view of Irving Peak to the north.

As you continue on you'll hike through meadows and aspen groves, with a few pine stands thrown in as well. The trail continues at an easy to moderate grade, crossing several small streams en route. At 9.3 miles you'll see a bridge across Vallecito Creek. This leads to the Johnson Creek Trail and Columbine Pass. (See Hike 5, Elk Park/Chicago Basin Shuttle-Loop for more information.)

After 11.4 miles you'll ford Roell Creek. At 12.9 miles you'll see some nice places to camp across from the Sunlight Creek drainage, where there are more wonderful views of the Needle Mountains. There are more nice places to camp in the area near the Rock Creek crossing at 14.8 miles. Be prepared to get your feet wet at this crossing.

Wonderful views continue as you hike through an array of wildflower-blessed meadows, then ford Vallecito Creek at 17.6 miles. Look for waterfalls, cascades, and pools just prior to and in this area. The trail begins to steepen as you proceed, paralleling Nebo Creek for a short distance.

After 17.9 miles you'll reach an unsigned trail junction on the right (east). This is the Continental Divide Trail, which heads over Nebo Pass, and eventually south to Mexico. Stay straight here; you will now be hiking the northbound Continental Divide Trail, which ultimately leads to Canada. The trail first goes to the headwaters of Vallecito Creek and Hunchback Pass, your destination if you so desire.

Cross Vallecito Creek again at 18.4 miles and continue the steep (sometimes very steep!) ascent to Hunchback Pass at 19.4 miles. Wildflowers and plant life are abundant here in summer, with paintbrush, marsh marigolds, bluebells, hellebore, and other flowering plants.

Options: You can make the sometimes steep climb to Nebo Pass, where you'll find quaint Nebo Lake. There's a grand view west to the Trinity Peaks and Storm King Peak, plus a spectacular view east to the Rio Grande Pyramid and the Window. If you opt to do so, you'll have to hike an additional 1.6 miles and ascend 930 feet to the pass.

Camping: Vallecito Campground is a fee area with drinking water and outhouses.

10 Pine River/Flint Creek Semi-Loop

Highlights:	Scenic lakes, wildflowers, and wildlife. A day hike along the Pine River, or a five- to six-day backpack into the high country.
Distance:	Up to 43.1 miles, semi-loop.
Difficulty:	Easy day hike; strenuous backpack.
Elevation gain and loss:	+5,342 feet, -5,452 feet.
Maps:	USGS Vallecito Reservoir, Granite Peak, Emerald Lake, and Granite Lake; Trails Illustrated Weminuche Wilderness.
Management:	Columbine Ranger District, San Juan National Forest.
Special restrictions:	Camping is not allowed within 0.25 mile of Little Emerald Lake or within 0.5 mile of the north shore and 0.25 mile of the east and south shores of Emerald Lake. Camp no closer than 300 yards from Flint Lake. Saddle/pack stock are not allowed to graze or stay overnight within 300 yards of Flint Lake.
Trail conditions:	Portions of trail are not maintained, and some sections are steep. High river crossings possible. Heavy use in some areas.

Finding the trailhead: Go about 18 miles east of Durango via U.S. Highway 160 and you'll reach the small town of Bayfield. From there, head north on paved Vallecito Lake Road (La Plata County Road 501). After 8.9 miles you'll reach a junction with La Plata County Road 240, another possible route if you're coming from Durango. Keep straight (north) on CR 501 for another 4.5 miles; a sign points the way to Vallecito area campgrounds.

Turn right (east) on Forest Road 603, which is paved as it crosses the dam but turns to maintained gravel beyond. You'll pass four Forest Service campgrounds—Old Timers, Graham Creek, North Canyon, and Pine Point—as you travel around the east end of Vallecito Reservoir. After 4.7 miles you'll then reach a resort area where there's an outfitter, campground, laundromat, and hot showers. Stay straight (north) through the resort, crossing Los Pinos—what the locals call the Pine River—on a covered bridge. Make a left (west) and go 0.4 mile, entering another resort where there are cabins and a store. Keep to the right (east) as you travel through the resort, crossing a cattle guard and merging with Forest Road 602 as you continue.

Pine River/Flint Creek Semi-Loop

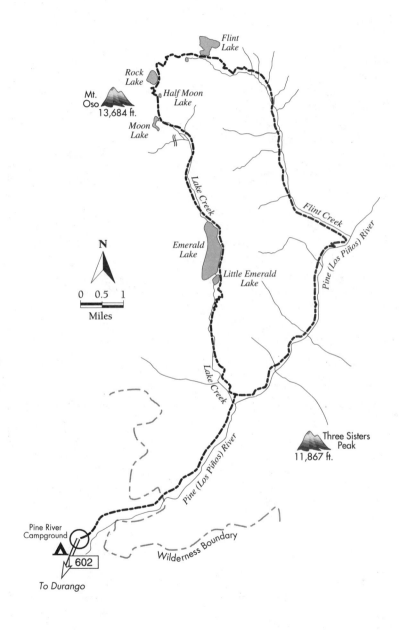

Flint
Lake

Rock
Lake

Half Moon
Lake

Mt.
Oso
13,684 ft.

Moon
Lake

Flint Creek

Lake Creek

Pine (Los Piños) River

N

0   0.5   1
Miles

Emerald
Lake

Little Emerald
Lake

Lake Creek

Three Sisters
Peak
11,867 ft.

Pine (Los Piños) River

Pine River
Campground

602

Wilderness Boundary

To Durango

It's an additional 3.8 miles to the Pine River Campground. Head through the camp to reach the trailhead in another 0.1 mile. You'll find plenty of parking, hitching posts, and an outhouse.

Key points
  2.7   Wilderness boundary.
  6.3   Lake Creek crossing.
11.0 Little Emerald Lake.
16.8 Moon Lake.
18.3 Top of ridge.
21.7 Flint Lake Trail junction.
29.9 Pine River Trail junction.
40.4 Wilderness boundary.

The hike: Enter through a private gate (please close it behind you) adjacent to Granite Peaks Ranch. This is private property. Camping is prohibited here, and you'll need to stay on the trail.

Aspens, ponderosa, and a variety of conifers will keep you company as you gradually climb along Pine River Trail 523. You'll see the Pine River, known locally as Los Pinos, off to the east as you begin. Later, trees and ranch sounds block the view and river sounds.

At 1.2 miles you'll cross Indian Creek. About 0.2 mile beyond this crossing, you'll pass through another gate; be sure to close it. The trail reaches a point near the river at 2.5 miles. It enters the San Juan National Forest in another 0.2 mile, then crosses into the Weminuche Wilderness.

Cross a huge rock outcrop at 3.2 miles. You can look for pika and marmots here. As you continue, you'll pass some meadows where you can find a place to camp in the trees. Although you will be heading away from the river at times, it is visible on occasion. Good campsites exist as you continue to the bridge crossing Lake Creek at 6.3 miles. Just beyond this crossing you'll see another camping place on the left. Though this is a scenic spot,

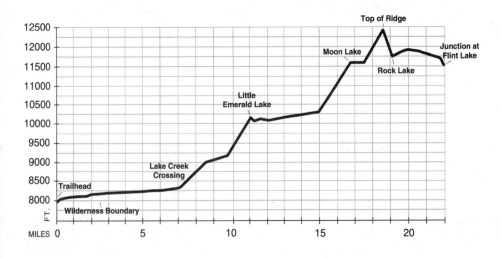

it's too close to the river. Hike another hundred yards or so and you'll see a better campsite on the right.

You'll soon reach the junction for Emerald Lake Trail 528. You'll have to cross a creek as you continue up the steep trail. Fortunately, the trail eases up a bit at the 8.6-mile mark. You'll cross a meadow, then pass a mecca of aspens, false hellebore, and an array of wildflowers by the time you reach 8.8 miles.

You must ford a creek at 9 miles, then hike gradually through dense woods alongside Lake Creek. After 9.3 miles the trail heads across an open slope, then goes back into the woods. You'll do the same as you head across a similar area at 9.7 miles.

Now the climb resumes its steep ascent, switchbacking up through dense woods. You'll emerge from the thick trees at 10.2 miles to find young aspens and spruce sharing the landscape with various wildflowers. You return to the trees at 10.6 miles. Over the next 0.4 mile you'll see places to camp on the left. Sites are abundant. The next available stopping point is the north end of Emerald Lake, a long haul from here if you are tired.

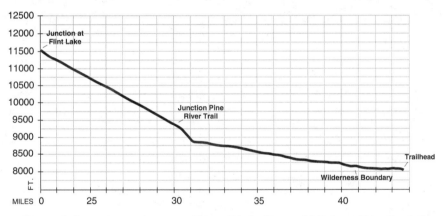

Beyond these campsites, you'll see Little Emerald Lake off to the left as you descend gradually. At 11.3 miles Emerald Lake itself appears, nearby and to the left. It's a beautiful place, one you'll want to spend time exploring. As the trail skirts the east edge of the lake, it climbs then drops 10 to 20 feet in turn, sometimes at a steep grade. This roller coaster continues past a number of small streams and a lovely wildflower-filled meadow to the north end of the lake, 12.9 miles from the trailhead.

Past the lake there are more creek crossings, including a ford of Lake Creek (high until late summer). If it's been a wet year you'll have a muddy trail to hike as you continue up the Lake Creek drainage. Still, there are numerous willows, the occasional moose, and an assortment of wildflowers to keep you amused. Best of all, you can camp 0.5 mile north of the lake and enjoy the area's beauty.

You'll make a gradual climb now as you head north, but the break doesn't last for long. Notice the waterfall on the left at 14.3 miles. In just 0.5 mile more you'll have to ford Lake Creek. The creek can be high until late summer.

Tarn above Flint Lake, after a thunderstorm.

A steep to very steep climb begins just prior to the ford, and from here the trail continually ascends, heading in and out of the trees. Along the way you'll pass assorted waterfalls, fording Lake Creek at 16.6 miles. In another 0.2 mile you'll come to Moon Lake with its lovely view of Mount Oso (elevation 13,684 feet). Campsites are limited at the lake. Deer and marmots frequent the area, so be sure to hang your food!

Although it isn't shown on maps, an unmaintained trail leads up and over the north ridge to Rock Lake. It's easy to follow, with rock cairns to point the way. Horses are not recommended on this route, however, since it is too steep and rocky.

At Moon Lake, ford the outflow and round the north shore. The slope here offers an abundance of wildflowers. After snowmelt you may see marsh marigolds, primroses, and glacier lilies. You'll reach the other end of the lake and the inflow creek after 17.2 miles. Don't cross this stream; instead, head up the steep drainage. After climbing for 0.5 mile you'll enter a rock field, cross a stream, and notice the mini hanging gardens. In another 0.2 mile you'll reach Half Moon Lake. This is a great place to look for ptarmigan. I saw a pair with some half-grown chicks. Although you won't find any places to camp here, Half Moon is a beautiful little lake and well worth a visit.

The trail continues upward on the west side of the lake, climbing at a very steep grade. At 18.2 miles you'll reach the head of a stream that flows into Half Moon Lake. Cross it and continue following the rock cairns to the top of the ridge, at 12,390 feet above sea level. From here you can see to Peters Peak to the northwest, and to Rio Grande Pyramid and The Window to the northeast.

This hike is best done after any snow has had a chance to melt off the north-facing slope. You'll head down from the ridge on a steep trail that could be slippery when wet or icy. At 18.6 miles, you'll come to a massive rock outcrop. There's a tiny lake on the right soon afterward. It had ice floating on it the day I was there—and that was mid-August.

Cross the lake outflow and continue down the steep trail through willows, flowers, and other dense vegetation. You'll soon reach Rock Lake and its plentiful campsites, at 19 miles.

The trail forks at 19.3 miles. The Rock Creek Trail takes off to the northwest. Head right instead to continue this loop. You will now be traveling the Flint Creek Trail 527. You'll begin climbing at 19.7 miles, where moderate to steep switchbacks lead to the high tundra and nearly level terrain. There's a lovely tarn just after you level off, and as you descend gradually you'll see other lovely pools. You'll come to a gentle ridge at 21.2 miles. If you step off the trail a bit, you'll have a view down onto Flint Lake.

Next you'll descend moderately into the trees. You can see the lake off to the left shortly thereafter. This area is for day use only, so you'll have to camp elsewhere. You'll reach a junction at 21.7 miles. The left (north) trail goes to Ute Lake; this trail also accesses the Pine River via La Osa. Keep straight to reach Flint Creek and the remainder of this loop.

The trail gradually descends to the 21.9-mile point, then begins a steep drop into the Flint Creek drainage. Later it eases off, descending moderately, and sometimes even ascending in and out of the trees and through a number of meadows. You'll cross many creeks en route. This trail can be a muddy mess during a rain. I experienced a 4-hour downpour here and saw a lot of water.

You'll have to ford Flint Creek at 24.8 miles. Just prior to the ford you'll see the remains of a huge mudslide that occurred in 1995. Fortunately, the trail was repaired and rerouted in 1996 by Vacation Volunteers and Forest Service crews.

There are several places to camp after the 26-mile mark. Around 27.7 miles the trail parallels Flint Creek, its waters cascading through the narrow canyon. You'll come to the junction of the Pine River Trail at 29.9 miles. There are more places to camp in this area.

From the junction, head right (south) to continue this loop and descend moderately. (Going left, or north, leads to the Continental Divide Trail.) Like many of the trails in this region, this one is deeply rutted in places. Please don't make matters worse by walking off to the side and making additional trails.

You'll soon descend into the textbook-like, glacier-carved Pine River realm, where there are abundant aspens and wildflowers. The route fords a creek at 31.2 miles. There's a camp nearby among aspens, and another closer to the river at 31.9 miles. Notice the tremendous waterfall off to the east as you continue downtrail. Falls Creek offers a double waterfall at about 32.4 miles.

You'll pass through an area rich in willows, then ford aptly named Willow Creek at 33.6 miles. From here, continue the gradual descent through this lovely valley, finding nice campsites along the way. You'll make several creek crossings before meeting the trail that leads to Emerald Lake at 36.8 miles. Continue straight and back to the trailhead at 43.1 miles.

Camping: The Pine River Campground, located at the trailhead, charges no fee; water is not available.

11 Pine River Trail

Highlights:	Wildlife and wildflowers along a scenic river with waterfalls. A day hike along the Pine River or a multiday backpack to Weminuche Pass and back.
Distance:	24.5 miles one-way.
Difficulty:	Easy day hike; moderate to strenuous backpack.
Elevation gain and loss:	+3,052 feet, -330 feet.
Maps:	USGS Vallecito Reservoir, Granite Peak, Emerald Lake, Granite Lake, and Weminuche Pass; Trails Illustrated Weminuche Wilderness.
Management:	Columbine Ranger District, San Juan National Forest.
Trail conditions:	Maintained trail, though first couple of miles cross private land. River crossing necessary. Heavy use in some areas.

Finding the trailhead: Go about 18 miles east of Durango via U.S. Highway 160 and you'll reach the small town of Bayfield. From there, head north on paved Vallecito Lake Road (La Plata County Road 501). After 8.9 miles you'll reach a junction with La Plata County Road 240, another possible route if you're coming from Durango. Keep straight (north) on La Plata CR 501 for another 4.5 miles. A sign points the way to Vallecito area campgrounds.

Turn right (east) on Forest Road 603, which is paved as it crosses the dam but turns to maintained gravel beyond. You'll pass four Forest Service campgrounds—Old Timers, Graham Creek, North Canyon, and Pine Point—as

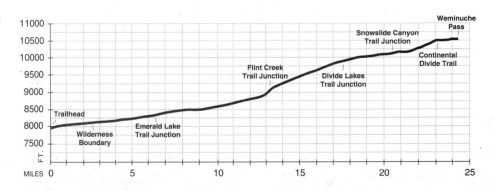

Pine River Trail

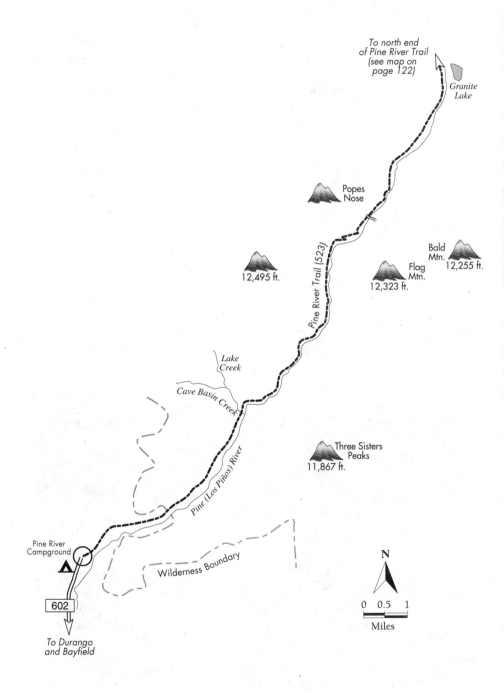

To north end
of Pine River Trail
(see map on
page 122)

Granite
Lake

Popes
Nose

Pine River Trail (523)

Bald
Mtn. 12,255 ft.

12,495 ft.

Flag
Mtn.
12,323 ft.

Lake
Creek

Cave Basin Creek

Three Sisters
Peaks
11,867 ft.

Pine (Los Pinos) River

Pine River
Campground

Wilderness Boundary

602

N

0   0.5   1
Miles

To Durango
and Bayfield

you travel around the east end of Vallecito Reservoir. After 4.7 miles you'll reach a resort area where there's an outfitter, campground, laundromat, and hot showers. Stay straight (north) through the resort, crossing the Pine River via a covered bridge. Make a left (west) in 0.4 mile, entering another resort where there are cabins and a store. Keep right (east) as you travel through the resort, crossing a cattle guard and merging with Forest Road 602 as you continue.

It's an additional 3.8 miles to the Pine River Campground. Head through the camp to reach the trailhead in another 0.1 mile. You'll find plenty of parking, hitching posts, and an outhouse.

Key points
  2.7   Wilderness boundary.
  6.3   Emerald Lake Trail junction.
13.2   Flint Creek Trail junction.
17.7   Divide Lakes Trail junction.
20.5   Snowslide Canyon Trail junction.
23.1   Continental Divide Trail.

The hike: Access the trail through a private gate (please close behind you) adjacent to Granite Peaks Ranch. This is private property. Camping is prohibited here, and you'll need to stay on the trail. Aspens, ponderosa pines, and a variety of conifers will keep you company as you gradually climb along what is sometimes a hot, dusty trail—Pine River Trail 523. You'll see Los Pinos, the Pine River, off to the east as you begin, but trees and ranch sounds soon block the view and river noise.

Donna Ikenberry on the Pine River Trail.

62

At 1.2 miles you'll cross Indian Creek. In another 0.2 mile is another gate; be sure to close it after you pass through. In just over a mile you'll come to a point near the river. You'll enter the San Juan National Forest in another 0.2 mile, then enter the Weminuche Wilderness.

The trail crosses a huge rock outcrop at 3.2 miles. You can look for pika and marmots here. Next you'll pass some meadows where you can find a place to camp in the trees. Although you will be heading away from the river at times, it is occasionally visible.

Good campsites may be found near the bridge crossing Lake Creek at 6.3 miles. Just after crossing you'll see another campsite on the left. While scenic, it's too close to the river. If you hike another hundred yards you'll see a better campsite on the right.

At this point you'll also reach the junction with Emerald Lake Trail 528. Keep going straight on the Pine River Trail. There are places to camp and several stream crossings as you climb to the junction with the Flint Creek Trail 527 at 13.2 miles. Along the way notice the abundance of aspens, willows, and summer wildflowers. There also are a couple of waterfalls to enjoy.

Beyond the junction you'll have to ford Flint Creek. Then continue ascending at a moderate, occasionally steep, grade to Pope Creek at 14.6 miles. Notice the busy beaver activity in this area. You'll cross another creek before the drainage opens up again. Posts mark the way across the Pine River to the Sierra Vandera Trail, heading east. You'll find some nice benches for camping near here, with a wide view to the north.

The trail now moves farther west of the river. A lovely grove of aspens keeps you company as you continue north. You'll cross more creeks on the way, including South Canyon Creek, before reaching the Granite Peak Guard Station at 17.5 miles. This guard station is manned by Forest Service personnel but is not open to the public. You can't see the station from the trail, only the fence. In another 0.2 mile you'll reach the trail leading east across the Pine River to Divide and Granite Lakes (Hikes 12 and 13). Continue straight (north) along the west side of the Pine River.

The valley narrows a bit as you hike through the trees; ford Cañon Paso at 18.6 miles as you continue to parallel the river. The trail climbs and descends, sometimes staying in the trees and sometimes heading out through a meadow. Campsites are available throughout the route.

You'll soon see a wonderful waterfall along the Pine River. In a short distance, at 20.5 miles, is the junction with the trail leading to Snowslide Canyon. The main trail continues to gently roll up to meet the Rincon de La Osa Trail at 21.3 miles. You'll have to ford the creek just beyond this junction.

You'll continue in and out of the trees for nearly a mile before you emerge into the biggest meadow yet. (It's about 2 miles long and at least 0.5 mile wide.) Your views are still blocked on both sides by mountains, but in the near distance you'll see an opening. This is Weminuche Pass.

You'll meet up with the Rincon La Vaca Trail, which is also the Continental Divide Trail (CDT), at 23.1 miles. The CDT heads west and east from here; wooden post-markers show the way. Keep going straight ahead. Ford the Raber Lohr Ditch in another 0.1 mile and continue north to the Continental Divide at Weminuche Pass, 24.5 miles from the trailhead.

Camping: Pine River Campground, at the trailhead, is free. Drinking water is not available.

12 Divide Lakes

Highlights:	Wildflowers and wildlife. The first 2-plus miles make a nice day hike. Otherwise, it's a two-day backpack. Trips to the East Fork Weminuche Trail and Granite Lake Trail are also possible.
Distance:	9 miles one-way.
Difficulty:	Moderate to strenuous.
Elevation gain and loss:	+1,560 feet, -810 feet.
Maps:	USGS Granite Lake; Trails Illustrated Weminuche Wilderness.
Management:	Columbine and Pagosa Ranger Districts, San Juan National Forest.
Trail conditions:	Maintained trail. High creek crossings are possible. Moderate traffic except during hunting season and early in the season, when it's heavy.

Finding the trailhead: From Hot Springs Boulevard and U.S. Highway 160 in downtown Pagosa Springs, head west on US 160. After 2.8 miles make a right (north) turn on Piedra Road (Forest Road 631). After 6.3 miles the pavement ends and the road becomes a well-maintained gravel route. In another 6.5 miles you'll reach a fork with Forest Road 633; keep to the left (northwest) on FR 631. Travel another 3.2 miles to the Piedra River. Just after crossing the river you'll come to another fork; keep to the left (north/northwest).

In 1.5 miles you'll reach the junction of Forest Road 636 and FR 631; stay left (north) on FR 631, passing Bridge Campground en route to the junction of Williams Creek Road (Forest Road 640) in 4.2 miles. Make a right (northwest) on FR 640, passing both Williams Creek and Teal Campgrounds.

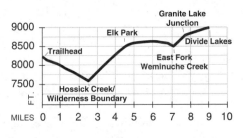

You'll reach another fork in 3.4 miles. Here, FR 640 goes right to the Williams Creek Trailhead; Poison Park Trailhead is to the left via Poison Park Road (Forest Road 644). Stay left (northwest) on FR 644. Drive another 3.1 miles to the trailhead at road's end; amenities are nonexistent.

Divide Lakes • Granite Lake • East Fork Weminuche Trail

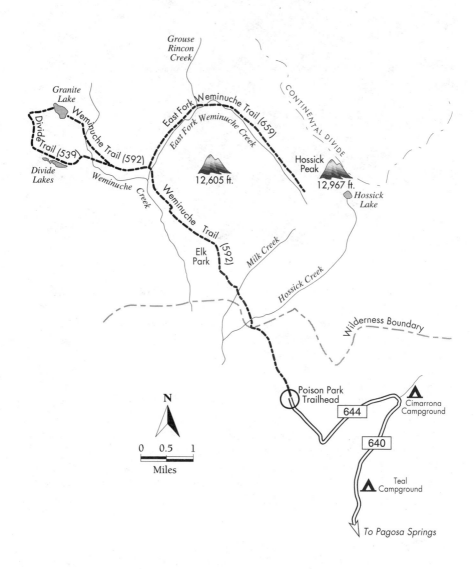

Key points

- 2.1 Junction with ranch fence.
- 2.4 Hossick Creek ford; wilderness boundary.
- 4.6 Elk Park.
- 7.0 East Fork Weminuche Creek ford.
- 7.8 Granite Lake junction on the right.
- 9.0 North end of Divide Lakes.

Divide Lakes at sunset.

The hike: Begin this hike on Weminuche Creek Trail 592; you'll start by crossing a large meadow of false hellebore and stunning summer wildflowers. The lush vegetation offers Colorado's state flower, the columbine, in addition to wild iris and many other species. Aspens and pines create a lush canopy. This hike is especially lovely from the trailhead down to the meadow just north of Hossick Creek. It's a great day hike, with moderate switchbacks leading you down to the meadow and then back up to the trailhead.

The trail remains pretty level for the first 0.8 mile, then descends moderately along the slope. Long, lazy switchbacks make the grade much easier. Along the way there's a stream crossing or two. You'll descend about 400 feet in 1.6 miles, then level off before descending a second time.

At 2.1 miles you'll come to a ranch fence that protects private property; please do not go beyond this fence. Instead, keep to the right, crossing the drainage ditch, and enter the trees. Ford Hossick Creek here (the crossing can be rough in early summer) to enter the Weminuche Wilderness.

Next you'll continue into a meadow. Ascend through the open area, watching for wildlife. Look for mountain bluebirds, robins, and turkey vultures, to name a few local birds. Leave the meadow and continue through the trees, crossing Milk Creek at 3.1 miles.

The trail climbs at a steep grade for nearly a mile, then levels off some. At 4.3 miles you'll head at what seems like straight up, going across a semi-open slope with pines, aspens, and lots of ferns. You'll reach level ground again at 4.6 miles, hiking through a mixed grove of young and mature aspens. This is Elk Park, a garden of grasses and wildflowers. You may see wildlife here, including elk. Bald Mountain is visible to the southwest.

As you hike along, the trail skirts the meadow and enters the woods now and then for nearly a mile. You'll have to make several small stream crossings as you go. Look for Granite Peak, which is to the northwest as you hike on. You'll cross another stream at 5.8 miles. Notice the number of blowdowns in this area. As you hike you'll see yellow signs that say "Center Stock Driveway" on occasion. At one time this route was used for moving sheep up into the high country.

At 6.3 miles you'll enter deep woods. Descend gradually, crossing another stream before reaching the East Fork Weminuche Creek at 7 miles. The remains of an old bridge wait at the crossing. Here you'll have to decide whether or not to ford the creek (which can be raging until mid-July) or cross on one of several logs. Whatever you decide, use caution!

There's a big meadow on the north side of the East Fork, but horses are not allowed to graze in this meadow. There are places to camp in the nearby trees.

You'll see the East Fork Weminuche Trail (Hike 14) heading off to the right as you enter the meadow. Continue straight, entering the trees and walking to another expansive meadow at 7.3 miles. Cross it and climb to the junction of the Granite and Divide Trails at 7.8 miles. Take the left fork to Divide Lakes via Divide Trail 539.

At 8.2 miles you'll cross a meadow. There are two more creeks to ford before you reach the lakes, one at 8.3 miles. There are some nice places to camp here. Next you'll switchback up a moderate slope to 8.8 miles. Continue to the north end of the biggest of the Divide Lakes, 9 miles from where you started. There are places to camp here and on the west side as well. The smaller lakes are too swampy for camping, and too difficult to reach.

If you stay overnight, sit around the lake and watch the beavers. The night I was there one beaver continually swam back and forth, slapping its tail over and over again, entertaining me to no end.

Camping: You must pass Bridge, Williams Creek, and Teal Campgrounds en route to the trailhead. All are fee areas with water and outhouses.

13 Granite Lake

Highlights: Wildlife and wildflowers. This day hike or overnight backpack begins at Divide Lakes (Hike 12). Trails lead to both the west and east sides of the lake, but they don't connect.

Distance: 2.1 miles one-way (west side); 3.1 miles one-way (east side).

Difficulty: Easy to strenuous.

Elevation gain and loss: +410 feet, -110 feet (west side); +620 feet, -320 feet (east side).

Maps: USGS Granite Lake; Trails Illustrated Weminuche Wilderness.

Management: Columbine Ranger District, San Juan National Forest.

Trail conditions: Maintained trail with steep sections. Sees moderate use most of the year, heavy use during hunting season.

Finding the trailhead: Both west and east side trails begin at the north side of the largest of the Divide Lakes. See Hike 12 for directions to the trailhead and lakes.

Key points, west side

0.0   North side of Divide Lakes.
1.0   Fork; begin climb to Granite Lake.
2.1   Granite Lake (west side).

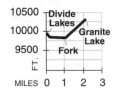

Key points, east side

0.0   North side of Divide Lakes.
1.2   Junction Granite Lake.
2.2   Weminuche Creek crossing (contained in hike).
3.1   Granite Lake (east side).

The hike: The west side of the Granite Lake Trail begins from the north side of the largest of the Divide Lakes, where you'll descend Divide Trail 539 to a junction at 0.5 mile. You'll pass the other lakes en route, but you won't see them unless you climb the ridge separating the trail from the lakes. Please note: This trail passes high above the lakes, making them difficult to reach.

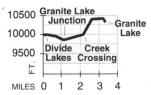

At the junction you'll find Trail 540, which leads to Granite Lake. Go right. At this point you are 0.1 mile east of the Pine (Los Pinos) River. The entire trail is not shown on some maps. From the junction, look for 12,323-foot Flag Mountain to the south/southwest.

Notice all the willows as you continue up the valley. This is a good place to look for moose. I saw three snowshoe rabbits here, their brown bodies and white feet hopping across the trail and on up a slope.

The trail stays mostly level for the first mile, then a sign points the way up—I mean *way* up—to the lake. This trail is steep with some slippery spots, so horses are not recommended. You'll climb to 10,280 feet above sea level at the 2.1-mile point. The trail then levels off as you near the lake.

You can camp on this side of the lake, with some nice campsites set among the granite boulders and slabs.

To hike on the east side of Granite Lake instead, hike east on Divide Trail 539 from the north side of Divide Lake, fording the creek. You'll reach the junction to Granite Lake at 1.2 miles. Head left on Weminuche Creek Trail 592, hiking up a moderate slope that can be steep at times. Cross a meadow and, at 1.8 miles, begin up a very steep slope. The trail is badly rutted in sections, which doesn't help. It does help, however, to concentrate on all of the lovely wildflowers seen in summer. These include paintbrush, wild strawberries, bluebells, a number of yellow composites, and many more.

After 2 miles the trail eases some, climbing gradually along Weminuche Creek, to the left. At 2.2 miles you'll ford the creek; notice the waterfall upstream. There's a trail fork immediately after this crossing. Both non-system trails (the Forest Service doesn't maintain them) lead to the same place. At the place they meet (about 100 yards away) you'll see another fork. One trail goes straight uphill. Take the other (left) fork, a cross-country route with nice views. You'll climb at a very steep grade, crossing the mostly open slope to a ridgetop at 2.7 miles. You get nice views as you climb of the enormous slab of granite on the left.

At 2.8 miles trails meet in a meadow. At 10,410 feet above sea level, this is the high point of this trail. Keep left (west) and at 3 miles descend one of several steep, rutted trails leading to the lake. You'll find places to camp around the water.

Camping: Divide Lakes; see Hike 12.

14   East Fork Weminuche Trail

See Map on Page 65

Highlights:	Wildflowers and wildlife. This is a two- to three-day backpack up the East Fork Weminuche Creek drainage.
Distance:	9.2 miles one-way.
Difficulty:	Moderate to strenuous.
Elevation gain and loss:	+1,790 feet, -950 feet.
Maps:	USGS Granite Lake; Trails Illustrated Weminuche Wilderness.
Management:	Columbine and Pagosa Ranger Districts, San Juan National Forest.
Trail conditions:	Maintained trail. High creek crossings are possible. Traffic is moderate except during hunting season, when it's heavy.

Finding the trailhead: From Hot Springs Boulevard and U.S. Highway 160 in downtown Pagosa Springs, head west on US 160. After 2.8 miles make a right (north) on Piedra Road (Forest Road 631). After 6.3 miles the pavement ends and the road turns to well-maintained gravel. Drive another 6.5 miles to a fork with Forest Road 633; keep to the left (northwest) here on FR 631. Travel another 3.2 miles, then cross the Piedra River. Just beyond the river you'll come to another fork. Keep to the left (north/northwest).

In 1.5 miles you'll reach the junction of Forest Roads 636 and 631. Stay left (north) on FR 631, passing Bridge Campground en route to the junction of Williams Creek Road (Forest Road 640) in 4.2 miles. Make a right (northwest) on FR 640, passing both the Williams Creek and Teal Campgrounds. You'll come to another fork at 3.4 miles; FR 640 continues right to the Williams Creek Trailhead; Poison Park Trailhead is to the left via Poison Park Road (Forest Road 644). Stay left (northwest) on FR 644. Drive another 3.1 miles to the trailhead at road's end; facilities are not available.

Key points
2.1 Ranch fence.
2.4 Hossick Creek ford; wilderness boundary.
4.6 Elk Park.
7.0 East Fork Weminuche Creek ford.
9.2 Grouse Rincon Creek crossing.

The hike: Follow the trail as described in Hike 12 a little more than 7 miles to the East Fork Weminuche Creek junction. The East Fork Weminuche Trail 659 is on the right upon entering the meadow. Head north, climbing gradually and moderately to the trees at 7.1 miles. The trail is very steep at times.

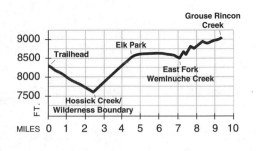

At 7.4 miles you'll level off, then descend. You'll have to cross many small streams in this section. Notice the views of nearby mountains and the creek drainage as you ascend. At 7.8 miles there's a wonderful view of a massive cascade on the East Fork Weminuche Creek. You'll make another stream crossing and get more ups and downs as you continue on. At 8.3 miles, look for a waterfall on the left.

You'll reach Grouse Rincon Creek at 9.2 miles. Ford the creek unless you are brave enough to cross via one of many downed trees. The trail leads right to a campsite at the 10,170-foot mark.

If you'd like to explore further, the trail continues another 3 miles or so. Please note that it is used mostly during hunting season; if you hike here in summer you should have it all to yourself.

Camping: You'll have passed Bridge, Williams Creek, and Teal Campgrounds en route to the trailhead. All are fee areas with water and outhouses.

15 Williams Creek to Williams Lake

Highlights: A hike to above treeline, with wildlife along the way. Good as a 3-mile day hike or a three-day backpack.

Distance: 9.8 miles one-way.

Difficulty: Strenuous.

Elevation gain and loss: +3,730 feet, -130 feet.

Maps: USGS Cimarrona Peak, Little Squaw Creek; Trails Illustrated Weminuche Wilderness.

Management: Pagosa Ranger District, San Juan National Forest

Trail conditions: Maintained trail with difficult creek crossings; moderate use.

Finding the trailhead: From Hot Springs Boulevard and U.S. Highway 160 in downtown Pagosa Springs, head west on US 160. After 2.8 miles make a right (north) on Piedra Road (Forest Road 631). In 6.3 miles the pavement ends and the road turns to well-maintained gravel. Drive another 6.5 miles to reach a fork with Forest Road 633; keep left (northwest) here on FR 631. Travel another 3.2 miles, then cross the Piedra River. You'll come to another fork just beyond the crossing. Keep to the left (north/northwest).

After 1.5 miles you'll reach the junction of Forest Roads 636 and 631. Stay left (north) on FR 631, passing Bridge Campground en route to the junction of Williams Creek Road (Forest Road 640) in 4.2 miles. Make a right (northwest) on FR 640, passing both the Williams Creek and Teal Campgrounds. You'll come to another fork in 3.4 miles. Poison Park Road (FR 644) takes off to the left, while FR 640 continues right (northeast) to the trailhead. Stay right, passing Cimarrona Campground after 0.4 mile. You'll reach the Williams Creek Trailhead and parking area after an additional 0.8 mile. There's an outhouse at the trailhead and plenty of room to park.

Key points
0.2 Wilderness boundary.
2.0 Indian Creek Trail junction.
3.6 Williams Creek ford.
7.2 Williams Lake Trail junction.
9.3 Williams Lakes.

The hike: After signing in at the trail register, gradually climb along the Williams Creek Trail, entering the wilderness after 0.2 mile. You'll soon climb moderately— sometimes very steeply—to reach a nice view of Williams Creek and its unique

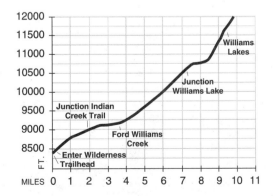

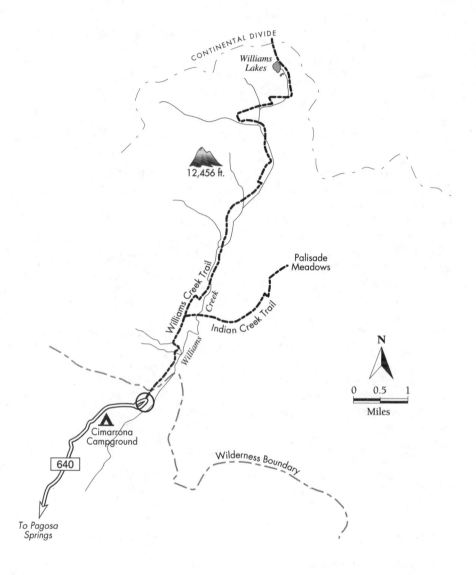

rock formations. Switchbacking even higher above the creek, you'll come to a stream crossing after 1.2 miles.

Continue on, crossing another stream at 1.4 miles. You'll reach the Indian Creek Trail 588 junction at the 2-mile point. If you'd like to hike to Palisade Meadows, turn here (see Hike 16 for more information). Hike 15 continues straight ahead through a meadow, then heads into the trees for a short distance. You'll cross several small streams en route and, at 2.2 miles, enter a big meadow. Circle around to the north end, where you'll enter the trees again and climb a ridge, topping off at 2.5 miles. Now descend along Williams Creek. You'll eventually ford it at 2.7 miles. You may need to remove your shoes and socks to do so.

After 3 miles of hiking, you'll descend a short distance. At 3.2 miles a spur trail goes off to the left; it leads to a bench along Williams Creek where there is a good place to camp. At 3.4 miles the trail enters a meadow and soon afterward fords Williams Creek. This crossing may be a bit easier than your last one, though there are no guarantees.

You'll cross another meadow at 3.8 miles and more streams at 4.2 and 4.8 miles. Aspens decorate the area, especially in fall when their vibrant colors brighten up the place. At the 5-mile point a spur trail leads near the creek and another campsite. The main route switchbacks upward. At 5.2 miles it passes some interesting rock formations, with lichen blanketing the rocks and pikas scampering about them. You'll cross a meadowy sideslope as you continue across several small streams.

After 5.6 miles you'll hike near Williams Creek again. Ford Williams Creek at 6.3 miles (there's a place to camp near the crossing), then cross the creek once more at 6.8 miles. You'll come to a junction with the West Fork Williams Creek Trail at 7.2 miles. The West Fork route (left) leads to the Continental Divide, but so does the trail to Williams Lakes. Keep to the right. You'll ascend on a steep grade, dropping a mere 30 feet to cross a stream at 7.7 miles. You'll then climb some more. The trail eases as you follow the contour line to cross two more streams at 8.3 miles. Though people have camped near here, the sites they have used are really too close to the water.

The trail continues, deeply rutted in places, as you make the very steep climb to several small lakes. The largest of the Williams Lakes is reached at 9.3 miles. If you'd like to continue on to the Continental Divide Trail at 12,000 feet, ascend another 0.5 mile on the steep grade to the top.

Camping: You'll pass Bridge, Williams Creek, Teal, and Cimarrona Camp-grounds en route to the trailhead. All are fee areas; all have water and restrooms.

16 Palisade Meadows

See Map on Page 72

Highlights: Wildflowers and wildlife on a nice hike along Williams and Indian Creeks. A long day hike or a nice two-day backpack.
Distance: 5.2 miles one-way.
Difficulty: Moderate to strenuous.
Elevation gain and loss: +2,450 feet, -150 feet.
Maps: USGS Cimarrona Peak and Palomino Mountain; Trails Illustrated Weminuche Wilderness.
Management: Pagosa Ranger District, San Juan National Forest.
Trail conditions: Maintained trail with some creek crossings; moderate use.

Finding the trailhead: From Hot Springs Boulevard and U.S. Highway 160 in downtown Pagosa Springs, head west on US 160. After 2.8 miles turn right (north) on Piedra Road (Forest Road 631). After 6.3 miles the pavement ends and FR 631 becomes a well-maintained gravel road. Drive another 6.5 miles and you'll reach a fork with Forest Road 633; keep to the left (northwest) on FR 631. After traveling another 3.2 miles you'll cross the Piedra River. At another fork just beyond the crossing, keep to the left (north/northwest).

After 1.5 miles you'll reach the junction of Forest Roads 636 and 631; stay left (north) on FR 631, passing Bridge Campground en route to the junction of Williams Creek Road (Forest Road 640) in 4.2 miles. Make a right (northwest) on FR 640, passing both the Williams Creek and Teal Campgrounds. You'll come to another fork at 3.4 miles. Poison Park Road (FR 644) takes off to the left, while FR 640 continues right (northeast) to the trailhead. Stay right, passing Cimarrona Campground after 0.4 mile. You'll reach the Williams Creek Trailhead and parking area after an additional 0.8 mile. There's an outhouse at the trailhead and plenty of room to park.

Key points
0.2 Wilderness boundary.
2.0 Indian Creek Trail junction.
2.3 Williams Creek ford.
5.0 Unsigned junction to the Continental Divide Trail.

The hike: After signing in at the trailhead register, hike Williams Creek Trail at a gradual grade. You'll enter the Weminuche Wilderness after 0.2 mile. Next you'll climb—sometimes at a very steep grade—to a nice view of Williams Creek and its unique rock formations. After 1.1 miles you'll start to switchback even higher above the creek. At 1.2 miles, you'll cross a stream, then another at 1.4 miles. You'll come to the Indian Creek

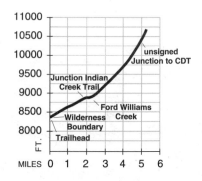

74

Blue grouse (Dendragapus obscurus).

Trail 588 junction at the 2-mile point. (You can continue up Williams Creek as a sidetrip; see Hike 15 for more information.)

Turn right (east) on the Indian Creek Trail. You'll descend here, eventually dropping about 90 feet to a stream at 2.2 miles. Hikers obviously camp at this crossing, but if you do, please camp away from the water. Continuing on, you'll soon ford Williams Creek. By summer's end you may be able to do so with your shoes and socks on, keeping your feet dry.

The trail climbs after the Williams Creek crossing, sometimes at a steep grade. Switchbacks help to make the grade more bearable. After 3.9 miles you'll ford Indian Creek; you'll cross yet another creek at 4.2 miles, then ford Indian Creek again at 4.7 miles. The trail gets very steep as you head up to an open slope beyond the ford.

After the 5-mile mark, you'll hike along Indian Creek to reach an unsigned trail junction. The junction comes about 100 yards before your route tops off at Palisade Meadows. From this point the Indian Creek Trail continues to the right (east), linking up to the Continental Divide Trail. The Palisade Meadows Trail continues north through Palisade Meadows and eventually connects with the CDT, too.

There are many nice places to camp in the trees surrounding this meadow. From this vista point, you can see the bald dome of an unnamed 12,153-foot peak to the north.

Camping: You must pass Bridge, Williams Creek, Teal, and Cimarrona Campgrounds en route to the trailhead. All are fee areas; all have water and restrooms.

17   Piedra Falls

Highlights: A short day hike to pretty Piedra Falls. Great for children.
Distance: 0.6 mile one-way.
Difficulty: Easy.
Elevation gain and loss: +40 feet, -20 feet.
Maps: USGS Pagosa Peak.
Management: Pagosa Ranger District, San Juan National Forest.
Trail conditions: Maintained trail, heavy use. Use extreme caution when climbing slippery rocks near the falls; a young girl fell and drowned here in the summer of 1998.

Finding the trailhead: From Hot Springs Boulevard and U.S. Highway 160 in downtown Pagosa Springs, head west on US 160. After 2.8 miles make a right (north) on Piedra Road (Forest Road 631). After 6.3 miles the pavement ends and FR 631 becomes a well-maintained gravel road. Drive another 6.5 miles to reach a fork with Forest Road 633; keep to the left (northwest) on FR 631. After traveling another 3.2 miles you'll cross the Piedra River. At another fork just beyond the crossing, keep to the left (north/northwest).

After 1.5 miles you'll come to the junction of Forest Road 636 and Middle Fork Road. Go right (northeast) on Middle Fork Road (also called Toner Road) for 1.8 miles. FR 636 continues north at this point, but you'll want to stay on Toner Road (Forest Road 637), which winds around to the east. At the junction, a sign points the way to Piedra Falls. Note: FR 637 is graded but not graveled; it can be slippery when wet.

You'll reach the trailhead and plenty of space for a primitive camp along the East Fork Piedra River in another 7.5 miles.

Key points
0.2   Trail climbs into the trees.
0.5   Trail exits the trees.

The hike: From the marked trailhead, follow the falls trail along the East Fork Piedra River for 0.2 mile. Another sign points the way at a trail intersection. You'll head into the trees (conifers and aspen) until the 0.5-mile point. After leaving the shelter of the tress, you'll reach the multitiered falls at 0.6 mile.

Camping: You can camp at the trailhead. It's free, but there are no facilities. If you want water and restrooms, try Bridge Campground off FR 631, just north of the FR 631/636 junction.

Piedra Falls.

Piedra Falls

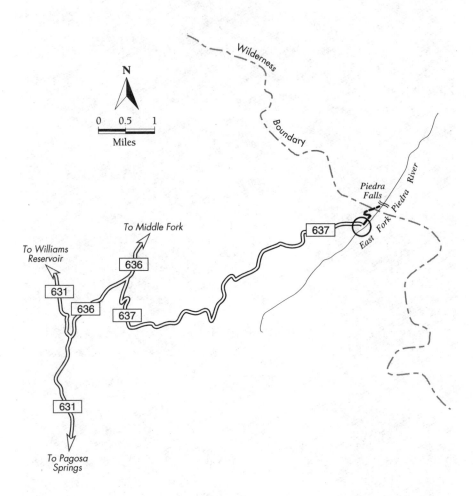

18 Fourmile Lake Loop

Highlights:	Wildflowers, wildlife, a scenic lake, and waterfalls. This is a long day hike or a nice two-day backpack up the Anderson Trail and down the Fourmile Creek Trail.
Distance:	13.2-mile loop.
Difficulty:	Moderate to strenuous.
Elevation gain and loss:	+2,680 feet, -2,590 feet.
Maps:	USGS Pagosa Peak; Trails Illustrated Weminuche Wilderness.
Management:	Pagosa Ranger District, San Juan National Forest.
Special restrictions:	Camping is prohibited within 100 yards of Fourmile Lake.
Trail conditions:	Maintained trail. High creek crossings are possible. There's light traffic on the Anderson Trail; heavy use on the Fourmile Trail.

Finding the trailhead: To reach the Fourmile Creek Trailhead, travel west on U.S. Highway 160 from the junction of Hot Springs Boulevard and US 160 in downtown Pagosa Springs. After 0.2 mile make a right (north) on Lewis Street. The road forks immediately; keep straight (north) on 5th Street North. Travel another 0.4 mile to the junction of 5th and Juanita Streets. Keep straight (north) here, driving on paved Fourmile Road (Archuleta County Road 400). After an additional 3.8 miles the road turns to maintained gravel. In another 3.5 miles the road becomes Forest Road 645, a narrow lane with turnouts. You'll enter San Juan National Forest soon after the name change.

Drive another 1.3 miles to a fork with Forest Road 634. Keep to the right (northeast) here on FR 645. You'll reach the end of the road and the trailhead after another 4.6 miles. There are no trailhead facilities.

Key points
- 0.9   Wilderness boundary.
- 4.4   Top of ridge.
- 5.3   Meadow.
- 7.3   Fourmile Lake.
- 8.3   Fourmile Trail junction.
- 10.4 Fourmile Falls.
- 12.6 Wilderness boundary.

The hike: At the trailhead, you'll find Anderson Trail 579 on the left and Fourmile Trail 569 straight ahead. Although you can do the loop in either direction (or forget the loop altogether and walk directly to Fourmile Falls, a popular destination), I opted to climb the Anderson Trail and descend via the Fourmile Trail. The Forest Service suggests you do the same due to the steepness and deteriorating condition of the old trail.

Head up the Anderson Trail, looking for wildlife such as elk and deer, and wildflowers such as bluebells, larkspur, wild roses, spirea, paintbrush,

Fourmile Lake Loop

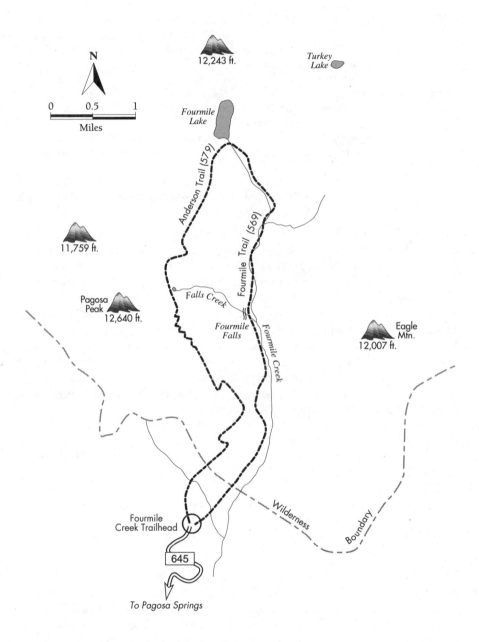

N

0   0.5   1
Miles

12,243 ft.

Turkey Lake

Fourmile Lake

Anderson Trail (579)

Fourmile Trail (569)

11,759 ft.

Pagosa Peak
12,640 ft.

Falls Creek

Fourmile Falls

Fourmile Creek

Eagle Mtn.
12,007 ft.

Wilderness

Boundary

Fourmile Creek Trailhead

645

To Pagosa Springs

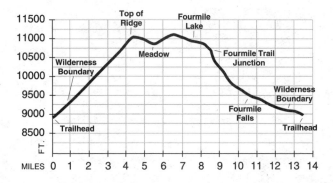

primrose, and marsh marigolds. You'll cross several streams as you climb the gradual to moderate slope. After about 0.4 mile there's a view to the south. You'll switchback up to a wilderness sign at 0.9 mile. At 1.1 miles you will be traveling through an area where aspens are predominant; it's a grand place come fall. Down the trail, pines and spruces take top prize.

You'll cross an open slope farther ahead, then it's back into the trees and more switchbacks as you continue up and up. At 1.8 miles look north to Pagosa Peak. After 3.5 miles you'll hike out across an open slope, a nice place to view the aftereffects of avalanches. You'll also have a close-up look at Pagosa Peak. The switchbacks continue, sending you back into the trees at 4.1 miles and up to the top of a ridge at 4.4 miles.

Next you'll descend through trees, traversing across numerous snow drifts if you're hiking early in the season. You'll enter a lovely meadow at 5.3 miles. There's a stream through the meadow, so if you want to camp here be sure to do so away from the water, where the vegetation isn't quite so fragile.

The trail climbs to 6.3 miles, then descends again, crossing a beautiful, wildflower-blessed stream at 7.1 miles. Continue to the 7.3-mile point, where you'll see Fourmile Lake. Set among enormous granite boulders, with wildflowers all around, the lake is a nice place for a picnic or campover. Please note that camping and grazing are not permitted within 100 yards of the lake.

The Anderson Trail continues beyond the lake, descending at a gradual to moderate grade for a while. It then steepens for a bit before reaching the Fourmile Trail junction at 8.3 miles. There's a place to camp near this junction. If you head east you'll reach Turkey Lake (see Hike 19); the loop described here continues south. You will now be hiking the Fourmile Trail.

Streams rush throughout the area early in the season, with the ground quite boggy at times. Prepare to get wet! At 8.4 miles you'll cross Fourmile Creek. Look for American dippers in this and other streams and creeks. These fascinating birds walk underwater searching for insect larvae and fish eggs. You'll hike near the creek then away from it, sometimes descending via a steep, rocky trail.

Notice the waterfall at 8.5 miles. In another 0.1 mile you'll cross Fourmile Creek. You'll be able to see another falls back up the creek as you cross again at 8.8 miles. There's another wonderful cascade on the left at 9.5 miles, and as you continue dropping steeply you'll see a double falls on the left. This is known locally as Upper Fourmile Falls.

Aspens on the Anderson Trail.

You'll come to Lower Fourmile Falls on the right at 10.4 miles. This is the most impressive of the falls along this trail, tumbling about 300 feet from cliffs to the rocks below. As you head on around the loop, you'll cross Falls Creek, which flows from the falls.

Fortunately, the trail eases as you hike south. As you travel, look to the east for a good view of the ragged crests of Eagle Mountain. You'll have to cross another creek, enter a meadow, then hike back into the trees before you've gone 12.5 miles. Exit the wilderness at 12.6 miles; the trailhead is just 0.6 mile farther.

Camping: There are various campgrounds in and around Pagosa Springs. Check with the Pagosa Springs Chamber of Commerce for more information.

19 Turkey Creek Trail

Highlights:	Wildlife and a scenic creek. Day hike the first few miles or make a four- to five-day backpack on the entire trail, the longest in this part of the wilderness. The Turkey Creek Trail can be combined with Hike 20, the West Fork San Juan Trail, for a shuttle-loop known locally as the Rainbow Trail.
Distance:	20.3 miles one-way.
Difficulty:	Moderate to strenuous.
Elevation gain and loss:	+4,600 feet, -1,540 feet.
Maps:	USGS Saddle Mountain, Pagosa Peak, and Palomino Mountain; Trails Illustrated Weminuche Wilderness.
Management:	Pagosa Ranger District, San Juan National Forest.
Trail conditions:	Maintained trail, with difficult creek crossings early in the season. Heavy traffic to Turkey Lake, light from Turkey Lake to the Continental Divide at Piedra Pass.

Finding the trailhead: Reach the Turkey Creek Trailhead by heading east from Pagosa Springs for 6.8 miles or southwest from South Fork for 25.6 miles via U.S. Highway 160. Go north onto signed Jackson Mountain Road (Forest Road 037), a dirt road. Drive 4.4 miles to the end of the road and trailhead.

Key points
5.2 Wilderness boundary.
8.3 Turkey Creek ford.
10.1 Fourmile Trail junction.
12.9 Rainbow Creek crossing.
16.5 Highest point along Turkey Creek Trail.
18.5 Meadow along East Fork Piedra River.
20.1 Continental Divide Trail.

Turkey Creek Trail • West Fork San Juan Trail

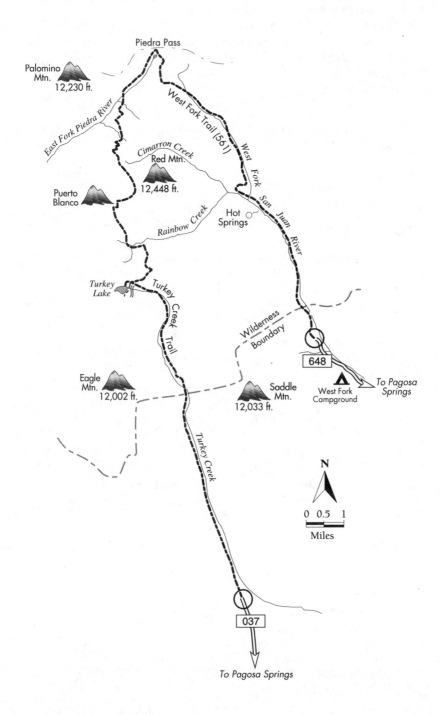

Piedra Pass

Palomino
Mtn.
12,230 ft.

West Fork Trail (561)

East Fork Piedra River

West Fork

Cimarron Creek
Red Mtn.
12,448 ft.

Puerto
Blanco

San Juan River

Rainbow Creek

Hot
Springs

Turkey
Lake

Turkey Creek
Trail

Wilderness
Boundary

648

Eagle
Mtn.
12,002 ft.

Saddle
Mtn.
12,033 ft.

West Fork
Campground

To Pagosa
Springs

Turkey Creek

N

0   0.5   1
Miles

037

To Pagosa Springs

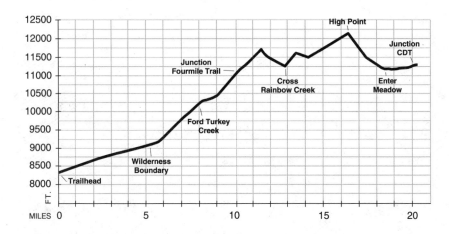

The hike: After signing in at the trail register, begin the gradual descent via the Turkey Creek Trail to a gate at 0.6 mile. After passing through this gate, be sure to close it. Soon after, you'll begin climbing a gradual to moderate grade, passing a spur leading to Turkey Creek and a place to camp. After 0.8 mile you'll have to cross an irrigation canal via a wooden plank bridge.

Be sure to enjoy the spruce and pine forest as you continue along. At 2.8 miles you'll cross a stream and hike across a lush meadow with a view of Saddle Mountain, 12,033 feet above sea level. You'll cross some more streams en route to the wilderness boundary at 5.2 miles. In another 0.1 mile you'll have to ford Turkey Creek. Expect to get your feet wet here almost any time of the year. There are places to camp, though they are too close to the creek and are reserved for outfitters in October and November.

At 5.7 miles you'll cross yet another creek, then begin a steep climb (moderate on occasion), crossing several more streams along the way. At 8.1 miles the trail flattens out some; it then fords Turkey Creek at 8.3 miles. There's a place to camp before this crossing.

Next you'll climb at a moderate grade across a semi-open slope until the 8.7-mile point, when the trail flattens and parallels a meadow. You'll ford Turkey Creek again at 8.9 miles. There's a nice place to camp near here. The trail crosses another stream at 9.2 miles and begins a steep climb. There's a nice waterfall on Turkey Creek after 9.3 miles.

You must cross several more streams en route to a junction at 10.1 miles. From here, you can reach the Continental Divide at Piedra Pass by continuing right (northeast) on Turkey Creek Trail. Go left (south) to reach Turkey Lake via Fourmile Trail; it's a mere 0.2 mile and a steep 100-foot descent to Turkey Lake, where you'll find some places to camp.

To finish the loop trail, go right. You'll climb a steep grade to the 11.2-mile mark, where you'll circle the first of several scenic basins. Look for wildflowers in early summer. Now it's a moderate 0.1-mile climb to the top of a ridge. From the ridgetop there's a grand view of South River Peak, Red Mountain, Sawtooth Mountain, and a whole lot more. Descend on a moderate slope, entering the middle basin where there's a little lake and some nice places to camp.

Piedra Pass area during a thunderstorm.

You'll reach a creek and a wooden post-marker at 11.7 miles. Soon afterward, you'll hike into the trees and then across a sideslope. After 12.4 miles the trail enters another basin, reaching the lowest part of the basin at 12.6 miles. Cross Rainbow Creek at 12.9 miles, then climb moderately to 13.4 miles and the top of the ridge. From here the route follows the elevation contour line, where there's an easy-to-moderate ascent past the steep walls of the massive rock formation known as the Puerto Blanco (White Door, in Spanish).

At 14.1 miles you'll cross another creek. Follow the wooden post-markers as you continue. If they're difficult to see, just aim for the ridge to the northeast. There are places to camp on the very scenic bench before you reach the top of another ridge after 15.1 miles. Nice views continue from this point on.

Continue hiking across the high, open plateau to 16.5 miles and the highest point along the Turkey Creek Trail. After enjoying the view, descend some very steep switchbacks to 17.4 miles and a creek crossing. There are places to camp in the area. It's a moderate descent to where you'll cross a stream, paralleling a vast meadow along the East Fork Piedra River.

Watch for wooden post-markers as you enter the meadow at 18.5 miles. Once out in the meadow you may find no post-markers, so cross the meadow to the north/northwest, aiming for the trees, crossing the East Fork Piedra along the way. Turkey Creek Trail is in the trees at 18.9 miles, along with a definite spur trail heading northwest up a drainage to Palomino Mountain. Stay in the trees, aiming northeast and up the East Fork Piedra drainage.

You'll cross a creek after 19.1 miles. You are now hiking through the meadow again, paralleling the East Fork Piedra River. Cross another stream or two en route to the junction with the Continental Divide Trail (CDT) at

20.1 miles. Signs point the way back to the East Fork Piedra River, Turkey Lake, and the Turkey Lake Trail. A CDT sign points the way west.

Continue on to Piedra Pass at 20.3 miles. This is a good place to camp. Just beyond is the junction to the West Fork Trailhead and the Rainbow Trail.

Options: If you're combining this trail with the West Fork San Juan Trail, see Hike 20 for additional information. The combined loop is 32.3 miles long.

Camping: East Fork Campground is about 4 miles north of Jackson Mountain Road off US 160 and Forest Road 667. It's a fee area with water and restrooms.

20 West Fork San Juan Trail

See Map on Page 84

Highlights:	Scenic river and hot springs, wildlife, wildflowers. A day hike if you concentrate on the first few miles of the trail, or a three- to four-day backpack to Piedra Pass. Can be combined with Hike 19 for a long shuttle-loop known locally as the Rainbow Trail.
Distance:	12 miles one-way.
Difficulty:	Moderate to strenuous.
Elevation gain and loss:	+3,620 feet, -360 feet.
Maps:	USGS Saddle Mountain and South River Peak; Trails Illustrated Weminuche Wilderness.
Management:	Pagosa Ranger District, San Juan National Forest.
Trail conditions:	Maintained trail. Heavy traffic to the hot springs; light traffic from the hot springs to Piedra Pass.

Finding the trailhead: Reach the West Fork San Juan River trailhead by heading east from Pagosa Springs for 13.6 miles on U.S. Highway 160, or southwest from South Fork for 18.8 miles via the same road. Turn north onto signed West Fork Road (Forest Road 648), a dirt road. You'll enter the San Juan National Forest after another 0.4 mile. Just beyond the boundary you'll see Wolf Creek Campground.

Continue 0.2 mile to a fork. Head left here toward the West Fork Campground, which you will reach in another 1.1 miles. Proceed another 0.6 mile and cross a bridge over the West Fork San Juan River. Keep right and continue to the trailhead, a mere 0.8 mile past the bridge.

Key points
1.6 Wilderness boundary.
2.9 Bridge over the West Fork San Juan River.
5.0 Hot springs.
5.6 First West Fork San Juan River ford.
8.1 Second West Fork San Juan River ford.
10.8 High point on ridge.

The hike: There's an outhouse and a registration box at the trailhead for West Fork Trail 561. From there, climb up the dirt road at a moderate grade, gaining 150 feet en route to the Born Lake Ranch entrance at 0.3 mile. Please close the gate behind you. You'll walk past three cabins, crossing an unnamed creek just before reaching the third cabin at 0.4 mile. Here the road forks (a sign marks the trail) to the right and continues past a small lake not visible from the trail.

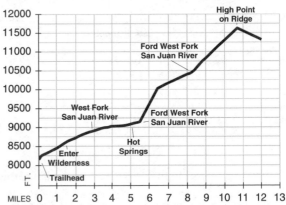

Views of the river are possible off and on beginning at about 1 mile. About the same time, you will find new joy in walking a trail instead of an old road. At 1.2 miles you'll enter the national forest. All the "Private Property Keep Out" signs will now disappear.

You'll mostly climb as you travel through lush vegetation. Although much of the trail is of a moderate grade, expect some short, steep sections. These are often easier to bear if you concentrate on the columbine, bluebells, wild strawberries, ferns, vine maples, and many other varieties of plants and flowers along the trail. Head away from the ridge overlooking the river and into a false hellebore-blessed meadow at 1.4 miles. You'll get views of some unnamed peaks nearby.

Michelle and Kurt hiking the West Fork San Juan Trail at Piedra Pass.

At 1.6 miles you enter the Weminuche Wilderness. Soon afterward, you'll cross a bridge over Burro Creek. You'll then enter another false hellebore-laden meadow at about 2 miles. Here there are more views of nearby peaks. As you head back into the trees, expect to cross some small creeks. The trail then switchbacks down about 30 feet to the West Fork San Juan River at 2.7 miles.

At 2.9 miles you must cross the river via a wonderful wooden bridge. There are old campsite areas near both ends of the bridge, but these are too close to the water. Camping is no longer allowed here.

Continue through the trees to a bridge over Beaver Creek at 3.1 miles. A new portion of the trail continues north from this point, climbing at a moderate grade then gradually ascending to the Beaver Creek Trail junction, at 4.4 miles. The gradual climb and stream crossings continue to a heavily used camp area on a bluff above the hot springs at 5 miles.

The springs are several spur trails away. Rock barriers usually serve to keep the cold river water from mixing with the hot sulphur water. If you visit on a high river day, however, the cooler river will mix with the hot springs, making a dip in the pool less than delightful. Special regulations apply at this site, and there is no overnight stock use. Future regulations may include limited camping in designated sites only, with no campfires.

As you continue up the trail you'll pass an open meadow, gradually climbing to 5.6 miles. Next you'll have to ford the West Fork San Juan River. The crossing may be difficult in early summer.

From here, at a place near where Rainbow and Cimarron Creeks unite with the West Fork San Juan River, you'll climb some steep switchbacks to 6.4 miles and a nice place for a break. Drop over the ridge after you've rested, continuing high above the West Fork San Juan River. You'll hike through the trees, crossing a stream now and then. Although you'll mostly ascend at a moderate grade, you'll encounter some steep sections, too.

Drop to the West Fork San Juan River at 8.1 miles, fording the river again; there are places to camp as you hike on. You'll cross an occasional meadow but hike mostly in the trees. Some are marked with red tree tags as you continue.

Climb the moderate slope to another river crossing. This point, at 9.5 miles from where you started, is near the headwaters of the West Fork San Juan. The crossing should be fairly easy. The trail then continues in the trees and later goes across a semi-open slope (which can be slippery) to a ridge at 11,620 feet above sea level. From the 10.8-mile point, the trail winds around the slope, offering nice views of the East Fork Piedra River drainage as you continue across the slope and eventually into the trees. You'll emerge from the trees in time to meet the Continental Divide Trail (CDT) at Piedra Pass at 12 miles.

Options: If you're combining this trail with the Turkey Creek Trail, see Hike 19 for further information. The combined loop is 32.3 miles long.

Camping: You'll pass Wolf Creek and West Fork Campgrounds en route to the trailhead. Both are fee areas with water and restrooms.

21 South Fork/Archuleta Lake Semi-Loop

Highlights:	Scenic lakes and solitude. The first 3 miles make a wonderful day hike; the loop is a three-day backpack trip.
Distance:	19.9-mile semi-loop.
Difficulty:	Moderate to strenuous.
Elevation gain and loss:	+2,840 feet, -2,840 feet.
Maps:	USGS Mount Hope and South River Peak; Trails Illustrated Weminuche Wilderness.
Management:	Divide Ranger District, Rio Grande National Forest.
Special restrictions:	No camping, riding, grazing, picketing, hobbling, or tethering saddle and packstock within 300 feet of Archuleta Lake.
Trail conditions:	Some of the trail is not maintained, and high creek crossings are possible. Light traffic on the South Fork Trail; heavy use on the Continental Divide and Archuleta Trails.

Finding the trailhead: To reach the trailhead at Big Meadows Reservoir, drive southwest from the junction of U.S. Highway 160 and Colorado 149 in South Fork, taking US 160 for 11.7 miles. Turn right (southwest) on Big Meadow Reservoir Road (Forest Road 410), a well-maintained gravel road that's paved for the first 0.4 mile. After 1.4 miles there's a fork: Big Meadows Campground is to the left (south); Archuleta Trail and the reservoir—a state wildlife area and popular fishing locale—are to the right (west). Stay right and go 0.2 mile to another fork in the road. The trailhead and boat ramp are 0.1 mile to the left (west); Forest Road 430 is to the right (north). At the trailhead you'll find plenty of room to park. There's an outhouse for your convenience.

Key points
1.6 Wilderness boundary.
3.0 Archuleta Creek ford.
4.3 South Fork Trail junction.
5.8 Tributary of the South Fork Rio Grande.
8.8 Continental Divide Trail.
11.7 Spotted Lake.
12.4 Archuleta Lake Trail junction.
15.6 South Fork Trail junction.

The hike: Archuleta Trail 839 provides access for backpackers and day hikers intent on seeing a potpourri of cascades, falls, and swirling pools along the South Fork Rio Grande. For a shorter hike, you can hike in 3 miles and out again, gaining only 520 feet in elevation.

The trail first takes a gradual grade around the west edge of Big Meadows Reservoir. Along the way, look for wildflowers such as scarlet gilia, elephant

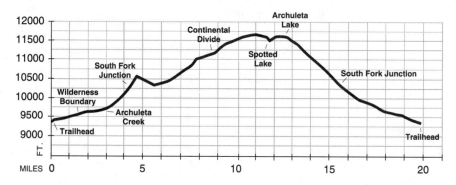

head, penstemon, bluebells, wild roses, and lots more. You'll cross a bridge at 0.4 mile. Later, at 0.8 mile, you'll reach the end of the reservoir. Continue on to where you meet the Loop Trail (on the left) at 1.1 miles. The main trail proceeds straight ahead (southwest) here, climbing along the scenic river. At 1.6 miles you'll enter the Weminuche Wilderness.

At the 3-mile mark you'll ford Archuleta Creek. This can be a tricky ford early in the season, so use caution. Next you'll climb a moderate to steep slope, sometimes via switchbacks. At 3.6 miles you'll cross Archuleta Creek again; ford another stream at 4 miles.

You'll come to the South Fork Trail junction on the left at 4.3 miles. If you've been sharing the trail with other hikers up to this point, you should now have the route all to yourself. The South Fork Trail is little traveled and offers plenty of solitude. You'll have to ford Archuleta Creek just after making a left. Then you'll begin to climb via some steep switchbacks to the ridgetop separating the South Fork from the Archuleta drainages. At 4.7 miles you'll start to descend the slope, which is quite steep at times.

At 5.3 miles the trail is fairly level. It remains at the same contour line as you cross several streams through this boggy area. In another 0.5 mile, you'll cross a tributary of the South Fork Rio Grande. This also can be a tough crossing, so use caution. Upon reaching the 6.2-mile point, you will begin traveling along the South Fork Rio Grande. It can be a raging river, a thrill to just sit and watch.

Soon after you leave the river, you'll cross a meadow. Watch for blazed trees as you continue or you might lose your way. Post-markers indicate the trail. Please note that early in the season, or after a rainstorm, the last 2 miles of the South Fork Trail can be awfully slick and boggy. Prepare to get wet if you don't have waterproof boots or socks.

You'll switchback up to the 7-mile point and find yourself back at the river. Numerous streams flow in the area, and you'll have to cross several creeks. You'll switch between meadows and trees as you continue, entering one last meadow and crossing another stream at 8.4 miles. As you make your way through this final meadow, post-markers help you across.

The eastern edge of this meadow is the beginning point for the Spruce Lakes Trail 710, which leads to the two Spruce Lakes. I couldn't find the trail junction, but if you follow the east edge of the meadow northeast a

South Fork/Archuleta Lake Semi-Loop

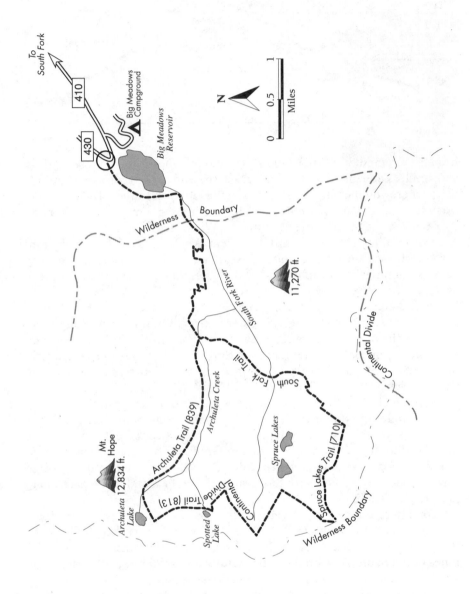

short way, you'll eventually see some blazed trees. Once you find the blazes it's a cinch to find the lakes. You'll climb about 80 feet or so, then descend a similar amount during the 0.7-mile hike to the lake. Camping is limited at the lakes; the surrounding areas are very boggy. You may find better campsites in the trees on the edge of the meadow.

After passing through the meadow, you'll enter the trees again. At 8.8 miles you'll reach the Continental Divide Trail 813. Make a right (north)

Spotted Lake at sunrise.

here, climbing a moderate to steep slope up into the trees. Along the way you can look back for a nice view of the South San Juan Mountains.

You'll reach a ridgetop at 9.5 miles. Hike along the open rock face here. The grade is nearly level as you cross several small streams, allowing you to enjoy the mountain scenery. After you've gone 10.8 miles the trail climbs more moderately. You'll reach the top of yet another divide at 11.2 miles. From here you can see north across the wilderness to the gray mass known as Mount Hope. This is the high alpine country of dreams.

Continue north across a vast talus slope. At 11.5 miles you'll begin to switchback down to Spotted Lake, another 0.2 mile away. You'll find places to camp on both sides of the outflow creek. You're near the Continental Divide here, so expect strong winds and fierce storms. The lake is beautiful, however, and worthy of a visit.

Watch for elk as you hike on to Archuleta Lake, climbing another 150 feet or so in elevation. After you've come up, the trail remains nearly level to the Archuleta Lake Trail junction at 12.4 miles. Turn right (east) here. Your route skirts the southern end of Archuleta Lake. It's best to camp in the trees so you won't harm the more fragile, open places. The latter are blessed with an assortment of wildflowers including marsh marigolds. You may not camp or picket, hobble, tether, or graze pack or riding stock within 300 feet of the lake. This distance may change—contact the Divide Ranger District for current regulations.

Beyond the lake it's a steep descent to Archuleta Creek at 13.1 miles. Cross the creek, then enter a meadow where the trail descends gradually. There are nice views of the South San Juans as you look ahead. You'll exit the meadow at 13.4 miles but enter another just 0.1 mile down the trail.

This enormous meadow graces the side slope for the next mile or so and makes the moderate to steep descent more bearable. Look for paintbrush, asters, Colorado columbines, bluebells, and an assortment of yellow composites among the wildflowers. Spruces add to the scene, as do marmots that go bounding down the trails, their heels kicking up a horse stampede of dust.

You'll cross some streams and descend several switchbacks as you continue your descent to 15-plus miles, where there are places to camp. You'll cross a semi-open slope at 15.2 miles. After that, it's back into the trees. From the 15.5-mile point it's a short, steep descent to the South Fork Trail at 15.6 miles. At the trail junction, head back the way you came in. You'll reach the trailhead after hiking a total of 19.9 miles.

Camping: Big Meadows Campground is located near the trailhead. It's a fee area with drinking water and outhouses.

22 Hope Creek Trail

Highlights:	Nice creek, meadows with wildflowers, wildlife. Good views of Mount Hope, Sawtooth Mountain, and the Continental Divide. A long day hike or overnight backpack.
Distance:	5.8 miles one-way.
Difficulty:	Moderate.
Elevation gain and loss:	+2,480 feet, -0 feet.
Maps:	USGS Mount Hope; Trails Illustrated Weminuche Wilderness.
Management:	Divide Ranger District, Rio Grande National Forest.
Trail conditions:	Maintained trail, moderate use.

Finding the trailhead: To reach the trailhead at Hope Creek, drive southwest from the junction of U.S. Highway 160 and Colorado 149 in South Fork, following US 160 for 11.7 miles. Turn right (southwest) on Big Meadow Reservoir Road (Forest Road 410), a well-maintained gravel road that's paved for the first 0.4 mile. After 1.4 miles you'll come to a fork. Big Meadows Campground is to the left (south), Hope Creek (a sign says Shaw Lake via Forest Road 430) is to the right (west). Keep right (north) at the next fork in 0.2 mile, driving FR 430 another 1.2 miles to the Hope Creek Trailhead. There is little room to park at the actual trailhead, but you can drive up the road a short distance and find a few more spaces.

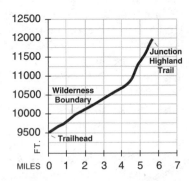

Hope Creek Trail • Kitty Creek Trail • Hunters Lake Loop • Highland Trail

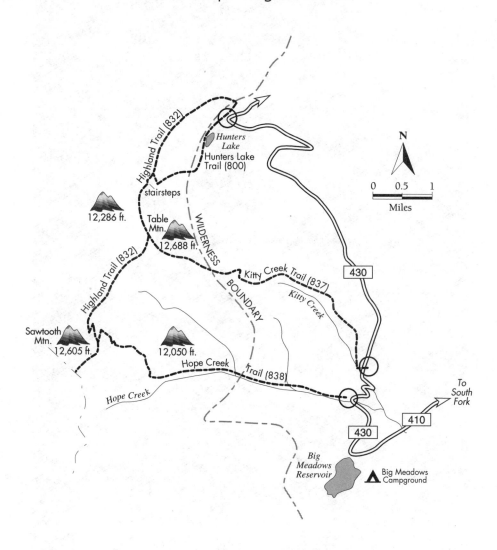

Key points

   1.3   Wilderness boundary.

   5.8   Highland Trail junction.

The hike: Sign in at the trail register, then begin hiking Hope Creek Trail 838. You'll travel through timber that allows nice views of Hope Creek. The trail grade is mostly easy for the first few miles.

Hope Creek Trail marker.

After 0.6 mile you'll cross a stream. You'll enter a meadow at 1 mile. In just 0.3 mile more you'll enter the Weminuche Wilderness. There are more stream crossings and more meadows to cross as you proceed. When the trail gets a little steeper, an occasional switchback helps ease the way. At 3.7 miles there's just such a switchback.

At 4.2 miles you'll cross a large meadow, gaining nice views to the south and west. After 4.9 miles the trail reaches a scenic basin semi-surrounded by mountains. By the time you've gone 5.6 miles, you'll reach the treeline. There are nice but exposed places to camp in this open basin. The trail continues to meet the Highland Trail (also known as the Highline Trail) at 5.8 miles.

Options: You can combine this trail with Hike 23, the Kitty Creek Trail, and a 2.5-mile portion of Hike 25, the Highland Trail, for a long loop of 14.3 miles. This includes walking the road for 1.1 miles between the two trailheads. If you want to backpack, you can camp at various places along the Hope Creek Trail. Camping areas are limited along the Kitty Creek Trail.

Camping: Big Meadows Campground, located en route to the trailhead, is a fee area. The campground offers drinking water and outhouses.

23 Kitty Creek Trail

See Map on Page 95

Highlights:	Abundant wildlife and great views once you emerge from the trees near Table Mountain. A long day hike is best, since camping spots are limited.
Distance:	4.9 miles one-way.
Difficulty:	Moderate to strenuous.
Elevation gain and loss:	+2,640 feet, -0 feet.
Maps:	USGS Mount Hope; Trails Illustrated Weminuche Wilderness.
Management:	Divide Ranger District, Rio Grande National Forest.
Trail conditions:	The trail is sometimes maintained; light use.

Finding the trailhead: To reach the trailhead at Kitty Creek, drive southwest from the junction of U.S. Highway 160 and Colorado 149 in South Fork, going 11.7 miles on US 160. Turn right (southwest) on Big Meadow Reservoir Road (Forest Road 410), a well-maintained gravel road that is paved for the first 0.4 mile. After 1.4 miles there's a fork: Big Meadows Campground (fee area) is to the left (south); the Kitty Creek Trail (the sign says Shaw Lake via Forest Road 430) is to the right (west). Keep right (north) at the next fork in 0.2 mile, driving FR 430 another 2.3 miles to the Kitty Creek Trailhead at Shaw Lake. There is little parking space at the trailhead, so park at the lake where there is plenty of room, plus an outhouse. The trailhead is just across the road.

Key points

3.3   Wilderness boundary.

4.9   Highland Trail junction.

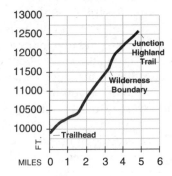

The hike: Sign in at the trail register. Kitty Creek Trail 837 begins through trees, mostly aspen for the first mile or so. Later you'll see pines, which are susceptible to windfall. Expect to cross many a fallen tree along this trail.

The trail is very steep in places. Follow switchbacks up to a tree-covered ridge, on which you'll stay for the first half of your hike. You'll cross Kitty Creek after 0.5 mile; you will not be seeing the creek again.

You'll come to an old logging road after 1.2 miles. Keep straight across this road, entering woods once again. The trail eases up some just before this road crossing, alternating between a fairly flat grade and a very steep one. You'll reach another old logging road at 2.2 miles. Cross it and continue.

After 2.4 miles you'll cross a creek. You're now heading southwest through some boggy areas. Look for elk and grouse as you continue. At 3.2 miles you'll emerge from the trees. Follow the post-markers and/or rock cairns up the slope to the west, which is very steep in sections. You'll pass stunted trees and tiny alpine wildflowers.

At 3.3 miles the trail enters the Weminuche Wilderness. Notice the faint trail heading southwest. Post-markers continue to mark your way, making life a whole lot easier. After another 0.3 mile you'll see post-markers to the northwest. Look back to see the Sangre de Cristo Mountains across the

View of the Weminuche from Kitty Creek and Highland Trail junction.

broad San Luis Valley. To the south see the South San Juans, and look southwest to Mount Hope and Sawtooth Mountain and the Continental Divide.

The trail eases, making for an easy to moderate climb with wonderful views to 4.9 miles and the Highland (also known as Highline) Trail. A sign points the way to the Continental Divide Trail, which you'll take if you want to connect with the Hope Creek Trail (Hike 22).

Options: Combine this trail with the Hope Creek Trail (Hike 22), and a 2.5-mile portion of the Highland Trail (Hike 25) for a long loop of 14.3 miles. This includes walking the road for 1.1 miles between the two trailheads.

Camping: Big Meadows Campground is located en route to the trailhead. A fee area, the campground offers drinking water and outhouses. Backpackers can camp along the Hope Creek Trail, though camping areas are limited along the Kitty Creek Trail.

24 Hunters Lake Loop

See Map on Page 95

Highlights:	Wildflowers and wildlife. The Hunters Lake Loop is a combination of two trails, the Hunters Lake Trail and a portion of the Highland Trail.
Distance:	4.2-mile loop.
Difficulty:	Easy to moderate.
Elevation gain and loss:	+620 feet, -620 feet.
Maps:	USGS Mount Hope; Trails Illustrated Weminuche Wilderness.
Management:	Divide Ranger District, Rio Grande National Forest.
Trail conditions:	Maintained trail with moderate traffic.

Finding the trailhead: To reach the trailhead at Hunters Lake, drive southwest from the junction of U.S. Highway 160 and Colorado 149 in South Fork. Take US 160 for 11.7 miles, then take a right (southwest) on Big Meadow Reservoir Road (Forest Road 410), a well-maintained gravel road that is paved for the first 0.4 mile. After 1.4 miles you'll come to a fork. Big Meadows Campground is to the left (south); Hunters Lake (the sign says Shaw Lake via Forest Road 430) is to the right (west). Keep right (north) at the next fork, in 0.2 mile. From there drive FR 430 another 9.6 miles to the Hunters Lake turnoff. Turn left (west) here. In 0.1 mile you'll reach the trailhead where there is plenty of parking and nice, big horse unloading ramps.

Key points
- 1.0 Wilderness boundary.
- 2.2 Highland Trail junction.
- 3.8 Unmarked trail junction.

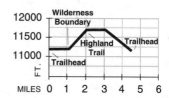

99

The hike: From the trailhead, Hunters Lake Trail 800 goes southwest through the trees and past a meadow on your left. You'll cross a stream at 0.3 mile and reach the north end of Hunters Lake at 0.5 mile. The south end of the lake is about 0.2 mile farther; there are places to camp around the entire lake.

Watch for tree blazes and rock cairns as you head south. You'll eventually cross an open slope with Colorado columbine, bluebells, yellow composites, paintbrush, and many more flowers to brighten your day. You'll cross into the wilderness after 1 mile. At the same time you'll see an unsigned trail junction. This lefthand trail is the Lake Creek Trail, which descends to Shaw Lake. You passed the lake on your drive to the trailhead.

Your route continues to the right across a semi-open slope decorated with spruces and other trees. You'll head into the trees at 1.3 miles and climb moderately. At 2.1 miles you'll begin to switchback up to the Highland Trail 832 junction at 2.2 miles. Make a right (north) onto the Highland Trail to continue this loop. (If you'd rather hike the more scenic portion of the Highland Trail, see Hike 25 for details.)

The trail stays nearly level through the trees, entering a meadow at the 3-mile point. Posts and rock cairns mark your way. You'll exit this meadow and enter a smaller one before descending moderately at first, then gradually, to an unmarked trail junction at 3.8 miles. There are two post-markers, one on each side of the trail here. If you look to the right you'll see another post. Hike down to this post; you'll then be able to follow tree blazes and an easy-to-follow path.

You'll reach Hunters Lake Trail at 4.1 miles. (If you're doing the loop in reverse, you'll want to find this unsigned trail by looking for the pile of rocks on the north side of the main Hunters Lake Trail. At one time a post marked the spot, but it is no longer in place. Turn left, or east, onto the Hunters Lake Trail and head back to the trailhead at 4.2 miles.)

Camping: Big Meadows Campground is located en route to the trailhead. A fee area, the campground offers drinking water and outhouses.

25 Highland Trail

See Map on Page 95

Highlights: Wildflowers, wildlife, and grand views. Day hike to the top of the Stairsteps or do a longer hike to the Continental Divide Trail; make it an overnight backpack if you'd rather.
Distance: 6.4 miles one-way.
Difficulty: Easy to strenuous.
Elevation gain and loss: +1,580 feet, -480 feet.
Maps: USGS Mount Hope and South River Peak; Trails Illustrated Weminuche Wilderness.
Management: Divide Ranger District, Rio Grande National Forest.
Trail conditions: Maintained trails, with steep dropoffs at times; light traffic.

Finding the trailhead: To reach the trailhead at Hunters Lake, drive southwest from the junction of U.S. Highway 160 and Colorado 149 in South Fork, following US 160 for 11.7 miles. Make a right (southwest) on Big Meadow Reservoir Road (Forest Road 410), a well-maintained gravel road that's paved for the first 0.4 mile. After 1.4 miles there's a fork: Big Meadows Campground is to the left (south), Hunters Lake (the sign says Shaw Lake via Forest Road 430) is to the right (west). Go right. Keep right (north) at the next fork in 0.2 mile, driving FR 430 another 9.6 miles to the Hunters Lake turnoff. Turn left (west) and you'll reach the trailhead in 0.1 mile. There is plenty of parking plus nice, big horse unloading ramps.

Key points
1.0   Wilderness boundary.
2.2   Highland Trail junction.
3.1   Kitty Creek Trail junction.
5.6   Hope Creek Trail junction.

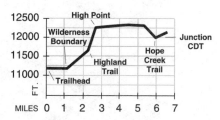

The hike: Hunters Lake Trail 800 begins through the trees and goes past a meadow, on your left, crossing a stream at 0.3 mile. You'll reach the north end of Hunters Lake at 0.5 mile. You'll see places to camp around the lake. The lake's south end is about 0.7 mile from where you began.

Watch for tree blazes and rock cairns as you head south, eventually crossing an open slope sporting a rainbow of summer wildflowers. Look for Colorado columbine, bluebells, yellow composites, paintbrush, and more here. You'll enter the Weminuche Wilderness at the 1-mile point; at the same time you'll see a trail junction. This is the unsigned Lake Creek Trail. It descends to Shaw Lake, which you passed on your drive to the trailhead. Keep going straight ahead to continue Hike 25.

You'll head across a semi-open slope of spruce trees. Hike into the trees at 1.3 miles and climb moderately. At 2.1 miles, you'll start to switchback up to the Highland Trail 832 (old signs still call this the Highline Trail) at 2.2 miles.

Indian Paintbrush and San Juan Mountains from Highland Trail.

At the trail junction, go left (south) and hike for 0.1 mile, continuing through to the trees to the beginning of what is known as the Stairsteps. These volcanic rocks are a joy to climb, with an assortment of lichens to enjoy. To the colorful lichens are added a wide array of wildflowers—columbines, asters, and phlox, to name a few. This place is pure magic. If you are afraid of steep places, try to keep your eyes on the lichens and flowers instead of the steep dropoffs.

You'll climb about 400 feet in just over half a mile, so expect the trail to be steep. Remember, once you're on top, the terrain levels off. At that point you'll have nothing to do but enjoy the see-forever views.

You'll reach the high point of the trail at about 2.8 miles. From there you can look down into the nearby meadow for elk, which are abundant. After a pause, follow the rock cairns across the nearly level plateau to reach another trail junction at 3.1 miles. You could head southeast from here to Table Mountain and the Kitty Creek Trail (Hike 23), but you'll probably want to stay high on the Highland Trail, traveling south toward the Continental Divide.

Continue following rock cairns to a point near Sawtooth Mountain at 5.2 miles. If you don't mind descending and ascending another 400 feet or so, switchback down to the junction of the Hope Creek Trail (Hike 22) at 5.6 miles. From there you can climb along the east side of Sawtooth Mountain to the Continental Divide Trail (CDT) at 6.4 miles.

Camping: Big Meadows Campground, en route to the trailhead, is a fee area; the price includes drinking water and outhouses.

26 Fisher Mountain

Highlights:	Nice views once you get on top of the mountain. Wildflowers and wildlife on a day hike.
Distance:	4 miles one-way.
Difficulty:	Moderate to strenuous.
Elevation gain and loss:	+2,127 feet, -70 feet.
Maps:	USGS Spar City; Trails Illustrated Weminuche Wilderness.
Management:	Divide Ranger District, Rio Grande National Forest.
Trail conditions:	The trail is easy to follow; light use.

Finding the trailhead: From Creede, drive southwest on Colorado 149 for 6.2 miles. Turn left (south) on Middle Creek Road (also known as Forest Road 523). Marshall Park Campground is just across the Rio Grande at the turn. Continue on, and after another 3.9 miles you'll reach a fork. Keep left (southeast) on Lime Creek Road (Forest Road 528). Go another 2.5 miles to a junction of Forest Roads 526, 527, and 528; keep to the right (southwest) as they all begin to merge. A road to Spar City continues straight (east).

Fisher Mountain • Ivy Creek Trail

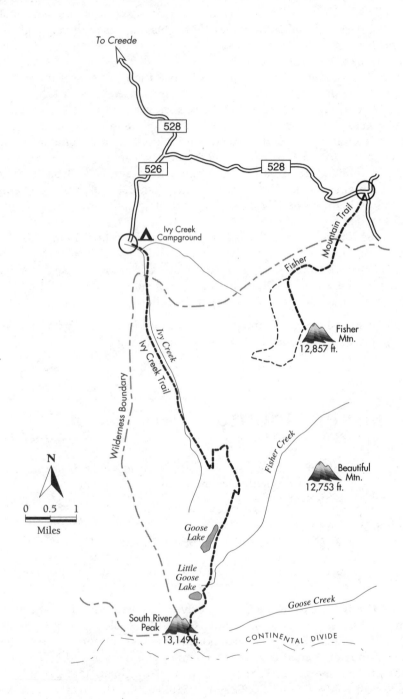

To Creede

528

526

528

Ivy Creek
Campground

Fisher Mountain Trail

Fisher
Mtn.
12,857 ft.

Ivy Creek

Ivy Creek Trail

Wilderness Boundary

Fisher Creek

Beautiful
Mtn.
12,753 ft.

N

0   0.5   1
Miles

Goose
Lake

Little
Goose
Lake

Goose Creek

South River
Peak
13,149 ft.

CONTINENTAL DIVIDE

Drive another 0.2 mile to reach another junction. Keep left on FR 528, then drive another 5.9 miles to the North Lime Creek Trailhead, on the right (south) side of the road. You can access two trails—Roaring Creek and Fisher Mountain—from this point. The Roaring Creek Trail takes off from the trailhead and leads the long way around to sites such as Goose Lake and the Continental Divide Trail. Our hike, the Fisher Mountain Trail, begins a short distance up Forest Road 440.

Key points
1.0   Wilderness boundary.
2.7   Deep Creek Trail (unsigned).

The hike: To reach Fisher Mountain, hike up FR 440, a four-wheel-drive road, for about 450 yards. You'll see a trail taking off to the right (south) and a sign pointing the way to Fisher Mountain Trail. Follow this sign.

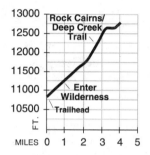

You'll first climb a moderate to strenuous grade along a ridge, hiking through trees. The Weminuche Wilderness boundary appears after about 1 mile. Continue on, reaching a nice view of Fisher Mountain after 2.2 miles. Next you'll hike along the edge of the trees for a short distance before entering the woods one last time.

You'll climb above treeline at 2.4 miles. At 2.7 miles, some rock cairns mark the unsigned Deep Creek Trail, which leads to Ivy Creek Trail and on to Goose Lake, about 8 or 9 miles south. Continue climbing straight across the open tundra to a plateau at 3.1 miles. The views are nice from here, but they're even better if you continue to the top of the mountain. You'll drop a bit before reaching the summit. You can see the Fisher Mountain Trail taking off along the west (right) side of the mountain.

To reach the top, continue climbing moderately over trailless terrain. The summit sits 4 miles from where you started, at 12,857 feet above sea level. I couldn't see much the day I was there (a storm blew in before my fiancé and I reached the top). But the 360-degree views have got to allow perspective on the Weminuche Wilderness and beyond. There's a trail register on top; be sure to sign it.

Options: You can do a 10-mile (plus or minus) loop at Fisher Mountain if you continue down the Fisher Mountain Trail for 1.5 miles to the Deep Creek Trail. After reaching the junction, head north/northeast on the Deep Creek route for 2.2 miles to the rock cairns at the 2.7-mile point of the description above. Then head back to the trailhead the way you came in.

Camping: You'll pass the Marshall Park Campground as you drive to the trailhead. It's a fee area; facilities include water, restrooms, and firepits.

27 Ivy Creek Trail

See Map on Page 104

Highlights:	Wildflowers and wildlife. This is the shortest and quickest access to Goose Lake.
Distance:	12.5 miles one-way.
Difficulty:	Strenuous.
Elevation gain and loss:	+3,690 feet, -90 feet.
Maps:	USGS Spar City and South River Peak; Trails Illustrated Weminuche Wilderness.
Management:	Divide Ranger District, Rio Grande National Forest.
Trail conditions:	An easy-to-follow trail; moderate use. High water crossings in early summer can be hazardous.

Finding the trailhead: From Creede, drive southwest via Colorado 149 for 6.2 miles. Turn left (south) on Middle Creek Road (also known as Forest Road 523). Marshall Park Campground is just across the Rio Grande at the turn.

Keep driving, and after another 3.9 miles you'll reach a fork. Stay to the left (southeast) here, on Lime Creek Road (Forest Road 528). Go another 2.5 miles to the junction of Forest Roads 526, 527, and 528; keep to the right (southwest) as they begin to merge. A road to Spar City continues straight (east).

If you drive an additional 0.2 mile you'll reach another junction. Proceed straight (southwest) on FR 526, heading to Ivy Creek. In another 0.8 mile you'll come to the junction of FR 527 and FR 526. Keep straight (south) on FR 526 to reach the Ivy Creek Trailhead and a primitive campground in 1.8 miles.

Key points
- 0.4 Wilderness boundary.
- 4.0 Ivy Creek ford.
- 6.5 Deep Creek Trail junction.
- 8.5 Goose Lake.
- 10.1 Little Goose Lake.

The hike: The Ivy Creek Trail begins through the trees and along the creek, climbing moderately to 0.4 mile where you enter the Weminuche Wilderness. You'll cross Ivy Creek after 0.7 mile. Then you'll skirt a meadow before entering the trees again at 1.6 miles. Switchback up at 2.2 miles, where the trail crosses a forested sideslope.

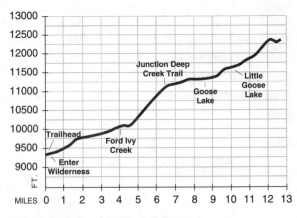

Goose Lake.

At 3.4 miles you'll cross a side creek; at 4 miles you'll have to ford Ivy Creek. Next you'll hike across a meadow, passing good places to camp in the nearby trees. Continue climbing moderately.

After 4.5 miles you'll enter the trees and climb a sideslope. Numerous switchbacks take you up as you go from trees to huge talus slopes, then back into the trees again. You'll reach a plateau and post-markers at 6.2 miles. Follow the faint trail and you'll reach the Deep Creek Trail at 6.5 miles. The Ivy Creek Trail continues south to Goose Lake; the Deep Creek Trail heads north, traversing the west side of Fisher Mountain (Hike 26).

Go south to continue this hike. You'll eventually hike back into the trees, climbing at a moderate grade. En route you'll pass a few rockslides, where you may see pikas. After 7.9 miles you'll descend to a stream. Afterward, you'll hike both in the trees and out of them, with good views into the Fisher Creek drainage as you continue across the wide bench. The trail drops to Goose Lake, where you will find plenty of nice places to camp, at 8.5 miles. Please remember to camp away from the shoreline.

To continue on to South River Peak, hike along the east side of the lake to its southern end. There you'll reach the Fisher Creek Trail junction at 8.9 miles. The Ivy Creek Trail continues south from this point, while the Fisher Creek Trail takes off to the south but turns north. Follow wooden post-markers as you head south on the Ivy Creek Trail, climbing a steep grade at times and crossing several streams. After 9.5 miles the trail eases up, following the contour line to Little Goose Lake at 10.1 miles.

You can find a place or two to camp at Little Goose; it's above treeline, so plan on using a stove. If you continue up the trail, numerous switchbacks lead up to the 11-mile point, where there's a rock cairn on the left (south). This is where the Goose Creek Trail merges with the Ivy Creek Trail. Continue upward via the switchbacks. At 12 miles you'll come to a nice spot just below the east side of South River Peak, which is 13,149 feet high. If you'd like, go on another 0.5 mile to the Continental Divide Trail.

Camping: Ivy Creek Campground is a primitive camp with an outhouse, but it's free. You can filter water from Ivy Creek. If you want amenities, stay in the Marshall Park Campground, which you passed en route to the trailhead. A fee area, it has water, restrooms, and firepits.

28   Fern Creek to Trout Lake

Highlights:	Solitude (once you're away from Ruby Lake); abundant wildlife.
Distance:	12 miles one-way.
Difficulty:	Moderate to strenuous.
Elevation gain and loss:	+3,380 feet, -580 feet.
Maps:	USGS Workman Creek and Little Squaw Creek; Trails Illustrated Weminuche Wilderness.
Management:	Divide Ranger District, Rio Grande National Forest.
Trail conditions:	Maintained trail; heavy use. The first 4.5 miles of trail are open to foot, horse, ATV, and mountain bike use. A large portion of the trail is above timberline; watch for afternoon thunderstorms.

Finding the trailhead: From Creede, go southwest on Colorado 149 for 16.3 miles. Turn left on gravel Fern Creek Road, also known as Forest Road 522. After 1.5 miles turn right at the sign for the Fern Creek Trailhead. There's plenty of parking and a hitching post for horses at the trailhead.

Key points
    4.0   Little Ruby Lake.
    5.1   Ruby Lake.
    5.7   Wilderness boundary.
    7.3   Jumper Lake Trail junction.
    9.7   Texas Creek Trail junction.
    11.1 West Trout Creek crossing near Trout Lake.
    12.0 Continental Divide Trail.

The hike: After you sign in, begin hiking Fern Creek Trail 815 through aspens and pines. Several long switchbacks make the initial climb a moderate one. After 0.7 mile you'll get a view to Antelope Park and the winding waters of the Rio Grande.

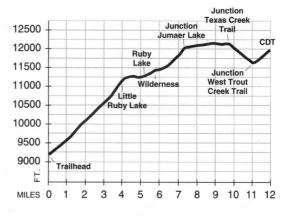

At 1 mile the grade steepens as you head up the Fern Creek drainage. You'll hike near the creek at times, but at other times you'll hike up above or away from it. After 2.7 miles you'll travel along the west side of a rockslide, a periodic flat area giving you room to breathe between some very steep sections.

Fern Creek to Trout Lake • Ruby Lakes/Red Lakes
Semi-Loop • Jumper Lake

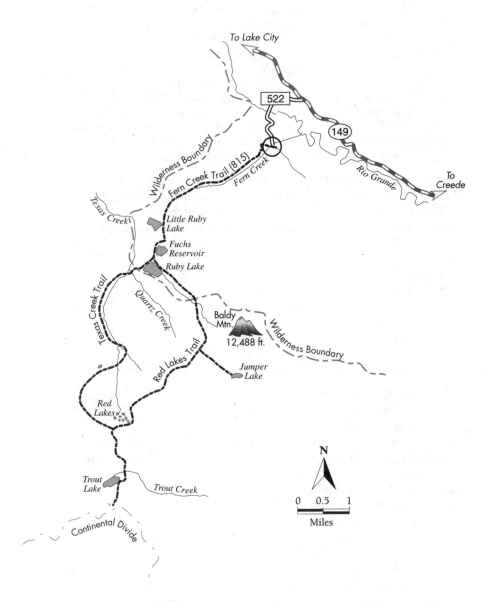

Continental Divide near Trout Lake.

The rock switches to meadow as you continue to a junction at 4 miles. The unmaintained Texas Creek Trail is off to the right. Look ahead to see Little Ruby Lake, a nice spot surrounded by meadow and trees, with some cabin remains on the lake's east side. Look for places to camp in the trees. As you continue across the flat meadow on the east side of the lake, you can see the high peaks in the northwest. It's a pretty view.

Head back into the trees at 4.2 miles. Next you'll climb at a steep grade. When you top off at 4.5 miles you can see Fuchs Reservoir on the left (south). Look for Chief Squaw Mountain (elevation 13,014 feet) to the southwest.

In another 0.2 mile you'll come to a trail junction. At the fork, go left (south) to continue to Ruby and Jumper Lakes. (The right fork follows the Fern Creek Trail/Old La Garita Stock Drive to Little Squaw Creek in 4 miles.) You'll reach Ruby Lake at 5.1 miles. You'll find the remains of several cabins there, one of which is fairly intact. There are nice camping sites around the old cabins and in the trees.

The trail forks at the lake. After visiting Ruby Lake, you can return to the trailhead via the Texas Creek Trail, which is to the right (west). (See Hike 29 for details on this 10.2-mile stretch.) The main route heads left (east) to a sign for the Red Lakes Trail, on the lake's northeast side.

At 5.7 miles you'll enter the Weminuche Wilderness. It's a moderate to steep climb from here up the drainage. There are nice places to camp along the way. The climb tapers off at 6 miles, climbing at an easy to moderate grade. After 7 miles you're up high enough to see west to The Window, the Rio Grande Pyramid, and other points of interest. Look for herds of elk in this region.

You'll reach an unsigned junction with the Jumper Lake Trail at 7.3 miles. Post-markers head southwest and southeast; Jumper Lake is to the southeast. To continue on to the Red Lakes, follow the post-markers southwest. You'll have to cross some little streams as you go across the nearly flat tundra. You'll climb gradually, however, reaching a small unnamed lake on the left (east) at 9.1 miles. The closest of the Red Lakes is on the right (west) at 9.2 miles. The lakes are really a pretty series of ponds surrounded by lush grasses. Here you'll find high and very exposed places to camp.

The hike proceeds to the unsigned junction with the Texas Creek Trail at 9.7 miles. If you continue south, you can overlook four unnamed lakes, then begin descending a very steep trail past wildflowers and lichen-covered rocks. Along the way look for pikas. Out in the distance you'll see Trout Lake and the Continental Divide at the Knife Edge, a narrow sliver of rock. As you descend you'll pass through thick stands of willows.

You'll cross a couple of small streams before you reach West Trout Creek at 11.1 miles. Continue on to an unsigned junction for the West Trout Creek Trail at 11.2 miles. Just beyond this crossroads, 100 yards or so, you'll see a pond on the left. Although you can't see Trout Lake from this point (you're too low), you can see spur trails that lead to the water and some campsites. Don't camp too close to the shore.

The trail will lead you around the east side of the lake. You'll view Trout Lake again as you begin the steep climb up to the Continental Divide Trail (CDT) at 12 miles. The CDT is 12,000 feet high at this point. This is also the junction for Williams Creek Trail. You'll find places to camp at Williams Lakes, just south of you (see Hike 15).

Options: This is a good way to reach the Continental Divide Trail (Hikes 36–39) near Trout Lake. You can also hike to and from Trout Lake, returning via the Texas Creek Trail. See Hike 29, Ruby Lakes/Red Lakes Semi-Loop, for more information. You can also make a side trip to Jumper Lake (Hike 30).

Camping: You'll pass Marshall Park Campground en route to the trailhead. It's 6.5 miles southwest of Creede, right off CO 149. The fee area includes water, restrooms, and firepits.

29 Ruby Lakes/Red Lakes Semi-Loop

See Map on Page 110

Highlights: Solitude (away from Ruby Lakes) and abundant wildlife. Day hike the first few miles of trail, or make a two- to three-day backpack to the high country.

Distance: 19.9-mile semi-loop.

Difficulty: Moderate to strenuous.

Elevation gain and loss: +3,230 feet, -3,230 feet.

Maps: USGS Workman Creek and Little Squaw Creek; Trails Illustrated Weminuche Wilderness.

Management: Divide Ranger District, Rio Grande National Forest.

Trail conditions: Maintained trail; heavy use. The first 4.5 miles of trail are open to hikers, horses, ATVs, and mountain bikes. A large portion of the trail is above timberline; watch for afternoon thunderstorms.

Finding the trailhead: From Creede, go southwest on Colorado 149 for 16.3 miles. Turn left on gravel Fern Creek Road, also known as Forest Road 522. After 1.5 miles make a right at the sign for the Fern Creek Trailhead. There's plenty of parking and a hitching post for horses at the trailhead.

Key points

4.0 Little Ruby Lake.
5.1 Ruby Lake.
5.7 Wilderness boundary.
7.3 Jumper Lake Trail junction.
9.7 Texas Creek Trail junction.
11.4 Small lake to the left (west).
13.8 Post-marker to Ruby Lake.
14.3 Wilderness boundary.
14.8 Ruby Lake.

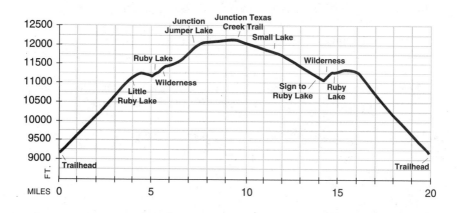

Backpack and old cabin at Ruby Lake.

The hike: After you sign in, begin hiking Fern Creek Trail 815 through aspens and pines. Follow the trail to the Red Lakes as described in Hike 28.

Proceed from there, and you'll come to an unsigned junction with the Texas Creek Trail at 9.7 miles. Post-markers lead the way as you turn and head around the Red Lakes, going generally northwest. The trail is faint or nonexistent at times, but if you look closely you'll find post-markers and rock cairns that mark the way. As you hike, look southwest for a closeup view of Chief Squaw Mountain and the Little Squaw Creek drainage.

After 11.4 miles you'll reach a small lake on the left. You'll also wonder which way to turn, since there aren't any visible markers or cairns, and the lake is not shown on maps. Head due east. You'll come to another post-marker at 11.6 miles. If you continue north, as others have done, you will find that the trail quickly fades away. You'll find a lone post-marker off to the north, but it marks another, unknown trail, not this one.

Beyond this point the trail is obvious at times, nonexistent at others. Don't worry, however, because post-markers and rock cairns do mark the way. You'll begin a gradual descent to the Texas Creek drainage, crossing a stream after 11.8 miles. A moderate descent soon has you paralleling Texas Creek, traveling through thick willows. Continue down a meadow, where there are good places to camp in the trees. You'll cross two branches of Texas Creek at 12.4 miles, hiking the east side of the creek for 0.1 mile until you cross back to the west side.

The trail heads out into the open, but still near the trees, as you cross a couple of streams and gradually descend. Good campsites can be found here. After 13.8 miles you'll reach a post-marker and sign pointing the way to Ruby Lake. Though you won't see a marker or cairn, there is a well-worn trail across the creek and up the hill. Follow it. You'll cross the meadow to the east, then ford Texas and Quartz Creeks before the 14.1-mile point, when you begin a steep climb.

You'll leave the wilderness at 14.3 miles. The trail lessens in severity after this point. You'll reach Ruby Lake at 14.8 miles. Head back to the trailhead the way you hiked in, reaching it after hiking a total of 19.9 miles.

Options: You may choose to spend time at Jumper Lake; see Hike 30 for more information.

Camping: Marshall Park Campground is on the road to the trailhead. It's 6.5 miles southwest of Creede, right off CO 149. It's a fee area; facilities include water, restrooms, and firepits.

30 Jumper Lake

See Map on Page 110

Highlights:	Lakeside solitude and abundant wildlife.
Distance:	8.3 miles one-way.
Difficulty:	Moderate to strenuous.
Elevation gain and loss:	+3,000 feet, -600 feet.
Maps:	USGS Workman Creek; Trails Illustrated Weminuche Wilderness.
Management:	Divide Ranger District, Rio Grande National Forest.
Trail conditions:	Maintained trail; heavy use. The first 4.5 miles of trail are open to hikers, horses, ATVs, and mountain bikes. A portion of the trail is above timberline, so watch for afternoon thunderstorms.

Finding the trailhead: From Creede, go southwest on Colorado 149 for 16.3 miles. Turn left on gravel Fern Creek Road, also known as Forest Road 522. After 1.5 miles make a right at the sign for Fern Creek Trailhead. There's plenty of parking and a hitching post for horses.

Key points
- 4.0 Little Ruby Lake.
- 5.1 Ruby Lake.
- 5.7 Wilderness boundary.
- 7.3 Jumper Lake Trail junction.
- 8.3 Jumper Lake.

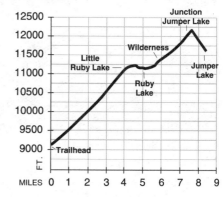

The hike: Sign the register, then begin hiking Fern Creek Trail 815 as described in Hike 28. Follow that route until you reach the unsigned

115

Porcupine (Erethizon dorsatum).

junction to Jumper Lake at 7.3 miles. At that point, post-markers head southwest and southeast. Go southeast to reach Jumper Lake.

It's a steep climb to the 7.5-mile mark and the top of a ridge. The Jumper Lake Trail winds down from here, switchbacking through willows. It's a steep, then later moderate, descent to the lake. You'll reach the shore at 8.3 miles. There are other ponds located nearby, and plenty of nice places to camp.

Options: You can combine this trail with Hike 29, the Ruby Lakes/Red Lakes Semi-Loop. Although you'll hike 19.9 miles instead of 16.6 miles round-trip, you'll see country you won't soon forget.

Camping: Marshall Park Campground is on the road to the trailhead, 6.5 miles southwest of Creede off CO 149. It's a fee area; facilities include water, restrooms, and firepits.

---

31 Squaw Pass

Highlights:	Wildlife, wildflowers, and colorful aspens come fall. A day hike along the first few miles, or a two- to three-day backpack to Squaw Pass and back.
Distance:	9.4 miles one-way.
Difficulty:	Moderate.
Elevation gain and loss:	+2,170 feet, -120 feet.
Maps:	USGS Weminuche Pass, Little Squaw Creek, and Cimarrona Peak; Trails Illustrated Weminuche Wilderness.
Management:	Divide Ranger District, Rio Grande National Forest.
Trail conditions:	Maintained trail; moderately heavy use.

Finding the trailhead: From Creede, drive southwest on Colorado 149 for 19.5 miles. Turn left (south) on Rio Grande Reservoir Road, also known as Forest Road 520. It's paved in the beginning, but after 0.5 mile the road surface turns to maintained gravel. Drive another 11.1 miles and make another left (south) at the signed junction for Thirtymile Campground and the Weminuche and Squaw Creek Trailheads. Keep right upon entering the area, reaching the trailhead parking area in 0.2 mile. If you're going into the wilderness on horseback, there's a stock unloading area 0.6 mile before the campground entrance. Stock unloading is not permitted in the campground.

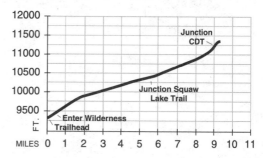

Squaw Pass

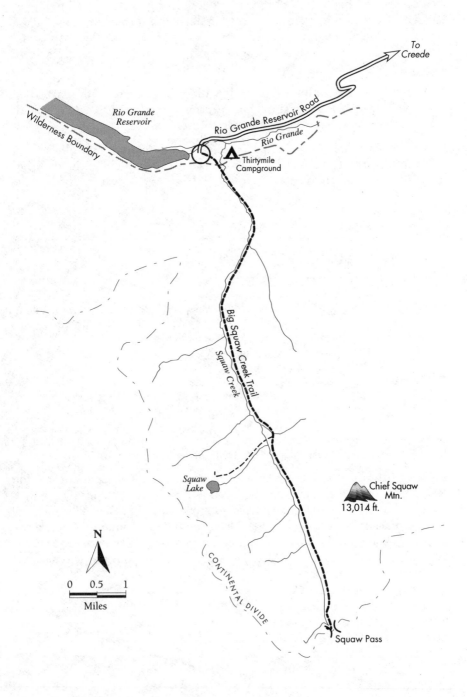

Key points
- 0.5 Wilderness boundary.
- 5.8 Squaw Lake Trail junction.
- 9.1 Continental Divide Trail.

The hike: After signing in at the register, head straight south on Big Squaw Trail. You'll soon be climbing through trees (conifers and aspens) at a moderate to steep grade. (Note: The trail heading right (west) from the register is the Weminuche Trail; see Hike 32.)

After 0.3 mile you'll see Squaw Creek off to the left. In another 0.1 mile you'll drop a bit, descending to a bridge across Squaw Creek at 0.5 mile. Just beyond, you enter the Weminuche Wilderness.

The trail climbs and occasionally descends as you follow Squaw Creek through a semi-narrow canyon. As you continue, the canyon opens up. You'll see an amazing array of colorful aspens here in the fall.

You exit the trees at 1.8 miles, ascending at an easy grade through vast meadows stretching to Squaw Pass. Along the way you'll cross many small streams, some with active beavers. At 5.8 miles you'll reach a junction and a bridge over Squaw Creek. The Squaw Lake Trail heads west over the creek and ascends a steep grade to Squaw Lake, which is 1,600 feet higher than you are. Your route continues south through the meadow, following wooden post-markers as you ascend. You'll occasionally hike amid trees, but expect to stay mostly in the open where you may see elk or even a moose.

After 8.4 miles the trail increases its pitch, climbing at a moderate to steep grade for 0.7 mile. You'll arrive at last at the unsigned junction where your route merges with the Continental Divide Trail (CDT). Wooden post-markers mark the way as you proceed south across a rocky slope. Look for pikas here. At 9.4 miles you'll reach Squaw Pass. From here the CDT takes off to the west and up a ridge, while the Cimarrona Creek Trail heads south to the Cimarrona Trailhead. The Cimarrona Creek Trail descends about 10 miles south to the trailhead, which is at 8,400 feet above sea level.

Camping: Thirtymile Campground is located at the trailhead. A fee area, it provides water and outhouses. River Hill Campground, also a fee area with water and outhouses, is 1.4 miles back along the road to the trailhead.

Johnna Heberling hiking Squaw Creek Trail.

32 Weminuche Pass

Highlights:	Lush meadows and wildflowers, plus access to the Continental Divide Trail.
Distance:	4.9 miles one-way.
Difficulty:	Moderate, although there are a few steep sections.
Elevation gain and loss:	+1,310 feet, -30 feet.
Maps:	USGS Weminuche Pass; Trails Illustrated Weminuche Wilderness.
Management:	Divide Ranger District, Rio Grande National Forest.
Trail conditions:	Maintained trail; moderately heavy use.

Finding the trailhead: From Creede, drive southwest via Colorado 149 for 19.5 miles. Turn left (south) on Rio Grande Reservoir Road, also known as Forest Road 520. It's paved in the beginning, but after 0.5 mile the road surface turns to maintained gravel. Drive another 11.1 miles and make another left (south) at the signed junction for Thirtymile Campground and the Weminuche and Squaw Creek Trailheads. Keep right upon entering the area, reaching a parking area in 0.2 mile. If you're going into the wilderness on horseback, there's a stock unloading area 0.6 mile before the campground entrance. Stock unloading is not permitted in the campground.

Key points

0.8   Wilderness boundary.
1.9   Bridge over Weminuche Creek.
4.9   Skyline Trail junction.

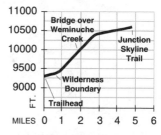

The hike: After signing in at the trailhead, which provides access to both the Squaw Creek Trail (Hike 31) and this trail, hike Weminuche Trail 818, going west toward the Rio Grande Reservoir. You'll hike past some old cabin remains after 0.3 mile, later passing the dam and spillway. You'll enter the wilderness in 0.8 mile.

The trail grade stays fairly level as you begin your hike, with some gentle ups and downs. At 1.3 miles you will begin hiking at a more moderate grade, with short, steep ascents through a mix of spruce and aspen. After 1.6 miles you'll turn south, heading up the Weminuche Creek drainage.

Cross a bridge over the creek at 1.9 miles, then continue climbing. At 2.1 miles the trail eases up some, climbing through some meadows ringed with aspen and spruce. You'll cross a couple of streams as you proceed, and some nice places to camp as well.

At 4.1 miles you'll have to ford an unnamed stream that flows from Simpson Mountain, to the west. Continue another 0.8 mile and you'll cross Weminuche Creek. You may have to get your feet wet here early in the season. Just after crossing Weminuche Creek you'll come to a junction with the Skyline Trail, which leads to The Window and the Rio Grande Pyramid. See Hike 33 for additional information.

Weminuche Pass • The Window

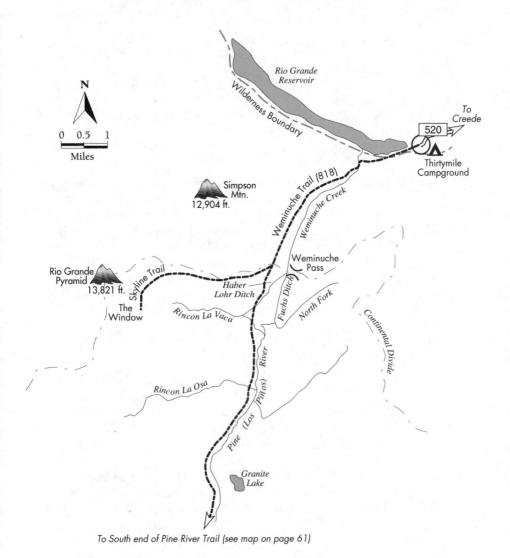

To South end of Pine River Trail (see map on page 61)

Options: At 10,630 feet above sea level, Weminuche Pass is the lowest point on the Weminuche portion of the Continental Divide Trail (CDT). If you're interested in connecting with the CDT you can hike the Skyline Trail and connect with the CDT near The Window (Hike 33), or you can continue south another 1.4 miles on the Pine River Trail (Hike 11).

Camping: Thirtymile Campground is located at the trailhead. It's a fee area; you'll find water and outhouses. River Hill Campground, also a fee area with water and outhouses, is 1.4 miles farther back down the road to the trailhead.

Weminuche Pass at Continental Divide.

33 The Window

See Map on Page 122

Highlights: Lush meadows, wildflowers, and grand views. Access to the Rio Grande Pyramid and the Continental Divide Trail.

Distance: 9.4 miles one-way.

Difficulty: Moderate to strenuous.

Elevation gain and loss: +3,080 feet, -130 feet.

Maps: USGS Weminuche Pass and Rio Grande Pyramid; Trails Illustrated Weminuche Wilderness.

Management: Divide Ranger District, Rio Grande National Forest.

Trail conditions: Maintained trail; moderately heavy use.

Finding the trailhead: From Creede, drive southwest via Colorado 149 for 19.5 miles. Turn left (south) on Rio Grande Reservoir Road, also known as Forest Road 520. It's paved in the beginning, but after 0.5 mile turns to maintained gravel. Drive another 11.1 miles and make another left (south) at the signed junction for Thirtymile Campground and the Weminuche and Squaw Creek Trailheads. Keep right upon entering the area, reaching a parking area in 0.2 mile. If you're going into the wilderness on horseback, use the stock unloading area 0.6 mile before the campground entrance.

Key points

0.8   Wilderness boundary.
1.9   Bridge over Weminuche Creek.
4.9   Skyline Trail junction.
8.5   Spur trail to Rio Grande Pyramid.

The hike: After signing in at the register, go west toward the Rio Grande Reservoir. You'll hike past some cabin remains after 0.3 mile, then pass the dam and spillway. Enter the wilderness in 0.8 mile.

The trail stays fairly level as you begin your hike, with some gentle ups and downs. At 1.3 miles you will begin

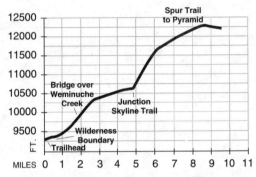

hiking at a more moderate grade, with some short, steep ascents through mixed spruce and aspen. After 1.6 miles you'll turn south, heading up the Weminuche Creek drainage. You must cross a bridge over the creek at 1.9 miles, then continue climbing.

At 2.1 miles the trail eases up some, climbing gently through some meadows ringed with aspens and spruce. You'll cross a couple of streams as you proceed, and pass some nice campsites as well. At 4.1 miles you'll have to ford an unnamed stream that flows from Simpson Mountain, to the west.

The Window and the Rio Grande Pyramid from Skyline Trail.

124

Continue to 4.9 miles and you'll cross Weminuche Creek. You may have to get your feet wet here early in the season.

Just after crossing Weminuche Creek you'll meet the Skyline Trail, which leads to the Rio Grande Pyramid and the landmark rock formation known as The Window. This is Weminuche Pass, at 10,630 feet above sea level; it's the lowest point on the Weminuche portion of the Continental Divide Trail (CDT). Marked by wooden post-markers, the CDT is actually 1.4 miles south via the Pine River Trail (Hike 11). (You could also reach the CDT by hiking the Skyline Trail to this junction near The Window.)

To continue on to The Window and the Rio Grande Pyramid, hike the moderate, though sometimes steep, trail through the trees. You'll soon head across a semi-open slope. You'll be able to look down into the vast meadow in the east on many occasions. After a while, you can look west to The Window and the Pyramid. The trail then eases up, passing through willows before reaching a tiny lake and good camping spot at 7 miles. From here you'll climb gradually, passing a spur trail leading to the top of the Rio Grande Pyramid (elevation 13,821 feet) at 8.5 miles. You'll reach the junction of the Skyline Trail and the CDT at a point near The Window after 9.4 miles total.

Camping: Thirtymile Campground is located at the trailhead. A fee area, it has water and outhouses. River Hill Campground, also a fee area with water and outhouses, is 1.4 miles back down the road from Thirtymile Campground.

34 Ute Creek Semi-Loop

Highlights:	Vast meadows, wildflowers, and wildlife, plus access to the Continental Divide Trail.
Distance:	25.2-mile semi-loop.
Difficulty:	Moderate, although there are a few steep sections.
Elevation gain and loss:	+3,200 feet, -2,860 feet.
Maps:	USGS Finger Mesa and Rio Grande Pyramid; Trails Illustrated Weminuche Wilderness.
Management:	Divide Ranger District, Rio Grande National Forest.
Trail conditions:	Maintained trail with moderate use. The river fording is dangerous until late summer.

Finding the trailhead: From Creede, drive southwest on Colorado 149 for 19.5 miles. Turn left (south) on Rio Grande Reservoir Road, also known as Forest Road 520. It's paved in the beginning, but turns to maintained gravel after 0.5 mile. Drive another 11.1 miles and you'll see a signed junction for Thirtymile Campground and the Weminuche and Squaw Creek Trailheads. Do not turn here. Instead, continue along the north side of the Rio Grande Reservoir for another 5.9 miles to a sign for the Ute Creek Trailhead. The

Ute Creek Semi-Loop

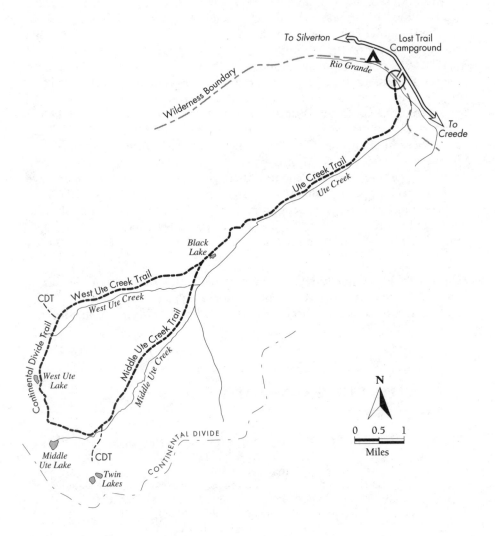

trailhead is on the south side of the road in 0.2 mile. There's an outhouse, a stock unloading area, and plenty of room to park or spend the night.

Key points

0.3   Wilderness boundary.
6.3   Black Lake.
7.2   East Ute Creek Trail junction.
9.3   Ute Lake Trail junction.
11.2   Continental Divide Trail junction.
14.2   CDT and West Ute Creek Trail junction.
18.6   Middle Ute Creek and West Ute Creek Trail junction.

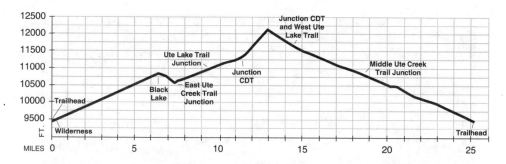

The hike: From the trail register, the Ute Creek Trail goes right along the river. Follow the signs, fording the Rio Grande after 0.1 mile. The crossing can be dangerous until midsummer.

From there, the trail climbs moderately. After entering the wilderness at 0.3 mile, you'll also enter thick groves of aspen. These can be absolutely gorgeous in late summer and early fall.

The trail takes a mostly gradual, sometimes moderate, grade as you continue, crossing a stream at 0.6 mile then heading up the Ute Creek drainage after 1.2 miles. An occasional switchback helps ease the way up. After 2.5 miles there's a great view up the Ute Creek valley to the high country.

Next you'll switch between hiking in the open and hiking in the trees (conifer and aspens), paralleling Ute Creek at times. You'll cross several streams before reaching Black Lake at 6.3 miles. There are places to camp in the area.

You'll come to a fork at 6.6 miles. Go left (south) to follow Middle Ute Creek. The right (west) trail heads up West Ute Creek; this will be your return trail for this loop. For now, hike south into the broad, vast meadows of the Middle Ute drainage, descending at a moderate to steep grade. You'll cross several creeks before you reach the East Ute Creek Trail junction on the left (southeast) at 7.2 miles.

At this junction, continue straight (south) on the Middle Ute Creek Trail. You'll keep climbing gradually to moderately, seeing The Window and the Rio Grande Pyramid to the east as you proceed. Though you'll hike mostly in the open, you'll pass through an occasional stand of trees. Your route crosses more streams as you climb to another junction at 9.3 miles. Here the Ute Lake Trail takes off to the left (southeast), while the Middle Ute continues straight (southwest). Hike straight up the Middle Ute to reach the Continental Divide Trail (CDT) junction after 11.2 miles. Newly rerouted, the CDT used to traverse the sideslope visible west of this point.

From the CDT junction you can head south to Twin Lakes (a mile or so away). If you wish to continue the loop, however, you'll need to climb the fairly steep trail to the 12.3-mile point. Here you'll meet the Middle Ute Lake Trail. Go right (north) to continue the loop. It's a moderate to steep climb to the ridgetop at 12.9 miles, where you'll get a grand view. You can see west to the Grenadier Range and other portions of the Weminuche.

Descend the slope, passing a little lake before reaching West Ute Lake at 13.5 miles. Please note that you must camp at least 300 feet from the lake; the best places are on the northeast side.

Donna Ikenberry enjoying the Middle Ute Trail—Rio Grande Pyramid in back.

When you're ready to proceed, continue to the junction of West Ute Creek Trail and the CDT at 14.2 miles. Keep straight (north) on the West Ute Creek Trail. You'll hike through the trees, descending to a vast meadow that extends down West Ute Creek for miles. There are many places to camp as you gradually descend. Be sure to look west to Nebo Mountain and Nebo Pass before you have gone too far.

You'll have to ford West Ute Creek after 15.2 miles. At 15.4 miles you'll come to a trail fork. From here you can climb to Starvation Pass, about 2 miles away; see Hike 35 for more information.

The trail crosses several streams and passes many nice places to camp as you descend to the Middle Ute Creek Trail, meeting it at 18.6 miles. From here you'll head back the way you came in, passing Black Lake and continuing on to the trailhead at 25.2 miles.

Camping: Thirtymile Campground is on the route to the trailhead. It's a fee area where you'll find water and outhouses. Lost Trail Campground is 0.8 mile beyond the trailhead turnoff, and also offers water and outhouses. It is free.

35 Starvation Pass

Highlights:	Stunning views, wildlife, and wildflowers.
Distance:	2.5 miles one-way.
Difficulty:	Moderate to strenuous.
Elevation gain and loss:	+ 1,200 feet, -0 feet.
Maps:	USGS Storm King Peak and Rio Grande Pyramid; Trails Illustrated Weminuche Wilderness.
Management:	Divide Ranger District, Rio Grande National Forest.
Trail conditions:	Maintained trail that is mostly above treeline. Moderate use.

Finding the trailhead: From Creede, drive southwest on Colorado 149 for 19.5 miles. Turn left (south) on Rio Grande Reservoir Road, also known as Forest Road 520. It's paved in the beginning, but turns to gravel after 0.5 mile. Follow it another 11.1 miles and you'll see a signed junction for Thirtymile Campground. Continue past this turnoff along the north side of the Rio Grande Reservoir for another 5.9 miles. You'll come to a sign for the Ute Creek Trailhead. Keep going straight.

From here, the road conditions change; the well-maintained gravel route becomes a narrow, bumpy, sometimes steep, four-wheel-drive road. If you have a good vehicle, drive another 0.8 mile to the Lost Trail Campground, then proceed an additional 8.5 miles to a junction for Stony Pass. A sign claims that the pass is 6 miles away via FR 520, while Beartown is 4 miles distant via Forest Road 506. Both are four-wheel-drive roads.

View to the north from near Starvation Pass.

Starvation Pass

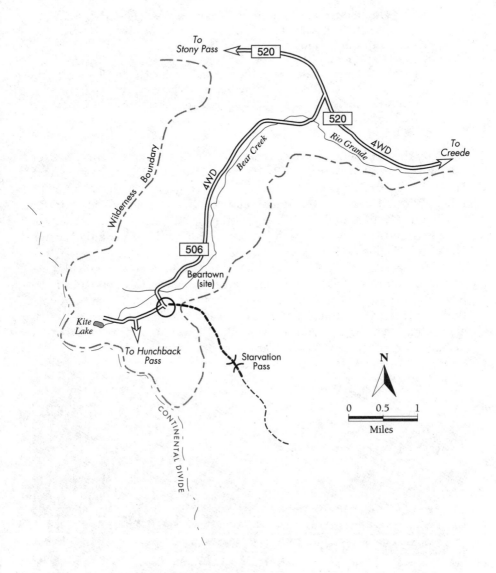

Turn left (southwest) on FR 506 and continue to the unsigned trailhead, which is just south of the old Beartown site. You'll drive another 5.1 miles, then turn onto a spur road taking off to the east. The road crosses two streams en route to the trailhead, another 0.2 mile away. If you reach the sign for Hunchback Pass you've gone too far. Turn around and head back 0.4 mile to the spur road.

Key points

  1.1 Emerge from the trees.

  2.5 Starvation Pass.

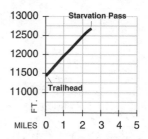

The hike: Although there isn't a sign pointing the way to the trail, there is a Weminuche Wilderness sign and a well-defined trail south of the parking area at road's end. Hike on this trail into the trees. Moderate to steep switchbacks lead the way for 1.1 miles. You'll emerge from the trees to terrific views. These begin as you climb the sometimes steep grade to the top of Starvation Pass at 2.5 miles. From here, you'll see many high peaks all around you. Look south to West Ute Lake, northwest to Stony Pass. The wonderful views are endless.

If you'd like to descend to the West Ute Creek Trail (Hike 34), with views of The Window and the Rio Grande Pyramid en route, continue another 2 miles or so. On the way you'll lose about 1,300 feet in elevation.

Camping: Thirtymile and Lost Trail Campgrounds are located en route to the trailhead. Thirtymile is a fee area with water and outhouses. Lost Trail is free, and also offers water and outhouses.

Continental Divide Trail

On its 3,000-mile journey from Mexico to Canada, the Continental Divide Trail crosses 85.7 miles of the Weminuche Wilderness, gaining a stunning 16,460 feet in elevation and dropping 14,476 feet over its route. It's a strenuous trail that is usually easy to follow. At other times, it's difficult to find or nearly nonexistent. It stays above treeline much of the way. Water may be scarce at times. Late afternoon thunderstorms can threaten hikers; snow can be deep in places, usually into July.

What to expect? I spent 10 days backpacking the Continental Divide Trail (CDT) with my husband-to-be, Mike, and we discovered one stunning vista after another. Starting at Wolf Creek Pass, we enjoyed hiking at an average elevation of 12,000 feet, surveying landmarks such as the Rio Grande Pyramid and The Window when we were still miles away. We also spied herds of elk, watched a ptarmigan and her babies, and delighted in a potpourri of colorful wildflowers. Imagine our joy at reaching Stony Pass knowing we had hiked 85.7 miles, and that a hot shower and Mexican food were in our near future! Though we were glad to reach our destination, at the same time we were both a bit sad to have to say goodbye to our high elevation odyssey.

July, August, and September are the best months for hiking the CDT, though you may encounter snow any month of the year. Hike too early in the season and you'll be postholing through thigh-deep snow. (The Forest Service claims some hikers have hit 20 foot drifts.) Worst of all, you'll miss the lovely wildflower display. Mike and I hiked the trail during the last part of July and hiked through little snow. We did encounter boggy sections, however, due to daily thundershowers that increased in severity as the days went by.

We hiked the entire Weminuche section of the CDT in one long backpack, but you don't have to do the entire trail at once. For your convenience, I've divided the trail into four sections, choosing what I think are the best places to link up and leave the CDT. You can hike them as I've suggested, or use your imagination and put sections together. You may want to link up with and leave the trail at other points. The choice is yours.

The sections are as follows: Hike 36, Wolf Creek to Sawtooth Mountain (13.2 miles); Hike 37, Sawtooth Mountain to Trout Lake (25.3 miles); Hike 38, Trout Lake to Weminuche Pass (19.5 miles); and Hike 39, Weminuche Pass to Stony Pass (27.7 miles). The hikes vary in miles but are similar in beauty. All are worthwhile hikes. Note: Though I've started the hiking miles at 0.0 for each segment, I've also noted the accumulated CDT miles in parentheses on the key points log. For example, the second segment begins at Sawtooth Mountain, which would show as 0.0 (13.2) under the key points heading.

Special note: When hiking the CDT, you'll sometimes find that water is scarce. Most of it is off the CDT a few hundred yards or a mile or so. Carry extra water while hiking through these areas.

36 Wolf Creek Pass to Sawtooth Mountain

Highlights: Stunning views, mountain lakes, wildlife, and wildflowers. A backpack trip, unless you want to hike a few miles out from Wolf Creek Pass and back again in a day.

Distance: 13.2 miles one-way.

Difficulty: Moderate to strenuous.

Elevation gain and loss: +2,850 feet, -1,340 feet.

Maps: USGS Wolf Creek Pass and Mount Hope; Trails Illustrated Weminuche Wilderness.

Management: Pagosa Ranger District, San Juan National Forest; Divide Ranger District, Rio Grande National Forest.

Trail conditions: The trail is easy to follow and above treeline some of the way; watch for late afternoon thunderstorms. Snow can be deep in places into July. Moderate use.

Finding the trailhead: The southern end of the Weminuche Wilderness portion of the Continental Divide Trail begins at Wolf Creek Pass. To get there, drive 22.6 miles east of Pagosa Springs on U.S. Highway 160. The unmarked trailhead is across from the sign for Wolf Creek Pass, elevation 10,857. A few wooden steps lead to the trail, which soon disappears into the trees.

If Lobo Overlook is open, save yourself a mile or so and gain 743 feet by driving to the radio tower and overlook. About 0.1 mile east of Wolf Creek Pass, look for a turnoff on the north side of the road. From here a gravel road leads to the 11,680-foot-high overlook, more than 2 miles away. There's a gate after 0.2 mile; if it's closed, you can park and walk.

Sawtooth Mountain is accessible from two nice trails. See Hike 22, the Hope Creek Trail, or Hike 25, the Highland Trail, to make your choice. If you like being up high, try the Highland route. Starting at the Hunters Lake Trailhead, it's the shorter (6.4 miles) of the two access trails, and climbs less (1,580 feet). (Note: It's 13.2 miles from Wolf Creek Pass to Sawtooth Mountain. If you were hiking out to or from the Hunters Lake Trailhead, you'd hike an additional 6.4 miles for a total of 19.6 miles.)

Key points

0.0   Wolf Creek Pass.
1.5   Trail junction from Lobo Overlook.
2.5   Wilderness boundary.
6.9   South Fork Trail junction.
10.5 Archuleta Lake Trail junction.
12.1 High point on ridge near Mount Hope.
13.2 Junction at Sawtooth Mountain.

Wolf Creek Pass to Sawtooth Mountain

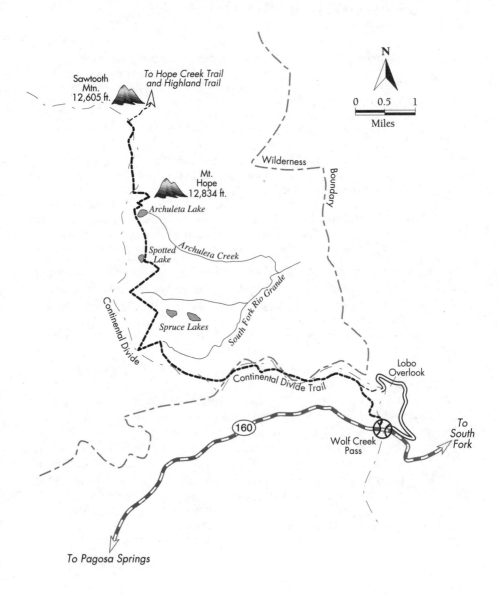

The hike: From Wolf Creek Pass, the Continental Divide Trail (CDT) begins on the north side of U.S. Highway 160. There's no trail sign, but a small series of wooden steps leads the way to the trail. You'll quickly move into the trees; switchbacks help make the moderate to steep climb a little easier to bear. The first rise tops off at 1.1 miles, where there are some nice views. You'll descend 40 feet or so before reaching the trail from Lobo Overlook at 1.5 miles.

You'll then climb again, to 1.6 miles. For the next 0.7 mile you'll descend a moderate to steep slope. Then you climb again for 0.2 mile, on an easy grade that takes you to the wilderness

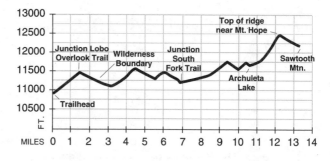

boundary. Next you'll descend and climb, rollercoaster-like, past a couple of meadows. You'll see a small lake on the left (and another on the right) at 5.4 miles. Set in rock, this is appropriately named Rock Lake. Most maps are incorrect, showing the lake farther to the west. It's a nice place to camp.

Beyond Rock Lake, the trail climbs at a steep grade to 5.7 miles. You now begin hiking off and on the true Continental Divide, always staying near the top. At 6.4 miles you'll be able to see Big Meadows Reservoir off to the northeast. You'll then descend along an eastern sideslope, crossing a large talus slope before heading back into the trees. The South Fork Trail junction appears at 6.9 miles.

Continue on the CDT, hiking across a meadow and into the trees. You'll climb at a moderate to steep grade. Long switchbacks, one descent, and an occasional stream crossing make the climb bearable. At 9.3 miles you'll come to a ridge above Spotted Lake. There are grand views of Mount Hope, the Hope Creek drainage, and more from this point. Traverse an open slope; it is decorated with wildflowers come summer. The trail switchbacks down to the lake at 9.8 miles.

Beyond Spotted Lake, you'll climb moderately past some meadows. Look for elk. You'll top a ridge at 10.2 miles, then descend gradually to a fork with the Archuleta Lake Trail. Continue north on the CDT to 11.1 miles, then switchback to the west. A series of steep switchbacks follows, offering grand views of both the South San Juans and the wilderness. You'll come to the top of a ridge at 12.1 miles. From here, Mount Hope's 12,834-foot summit seems close enough to touch.

To finish out this section, you'll descend easily to 13.2 miles and a junction with the Highland Trail (Hike 25) at Sawtooth Mountain.

Camping: Wolf Creek Campground is 14 miles northeast of Pagosa Springs, off Forest Road 648. It's a fee area; amenities include drinking water and outhouses. Big Meadows Campground is about 13 miles southwest of South Fork, off Big Meadow Reservoir Road (Forest Road 410). It's also a fee area, with drinking water and outhouses.

37 Sawtooth Mountain to Trout Lake

Highlights:	Spectacular views, high mountain lakes. Wonderful wildflowers plus wildlife, especially elk. A multiday backpack trip.
Distance:	25.3 miles one-way.
Difficulty:	Moderate to strenuous.
Elevation gain and loss:	+3,500 feet, -3,610 feet.
Maps:	USGS South River Peak, Palomino Mountain, and Cimarrona Peak; Trails Illustrated Weminuche Wilderness.
Management:	Pagosa Ranger District, San Juan National Forest; Divide Ranger District, Rio Grande National Forest.
Trail conditions:	The trail is easy to follow, but it's above treeline for some of the way—watch for late afternoon thunderstorms. Snow can linger in places, especially around the Knife Edge; use caution. Light to moderate use.

Finding the trailhead: Sawtooth Mountain is accessible from two lovely trails: Hike 22, the Hope Creek Trail, or Hike 25, the Highland Trail. If you like being up high, try the Highland route. Starting at the Hunters Lake Trailhead, it's the shorter (6.4 miles) of the two access trails and climbs less (1,580 feet). Note: It's 25.3 miles from Sawtooth Mountain to Trout Lake. If you are hiking in or out from the Hunters Lake Trailhead, you'll hike an additional 6.4 miles for a total of 31.7 miles. (If you choose to access Trout Lake from the Fern Creek Trailhead, add another 12 miles; see Hike 28.)

Key points

0.0 (13.2)	Sawtooth Mountain.
1.6 (14.8)	Sawtooth Trail junction.
6.5 (19.7)	High point along saddle.
9.4 (22.6)	Piedra Pass.
13.0 (26.2)	East Fork Trout Creek Trail junction.
21.2 (34.5)	Palisade Meadows Trail junction.
23.5 (36.7)	Cherokee Lake.
25.3 (38.5)	Trout Lake Trail junction.

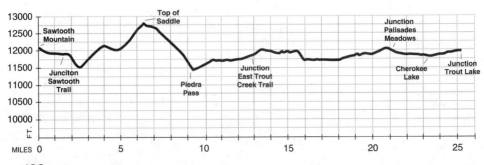

Sawtooth Mountain to Trout Lake

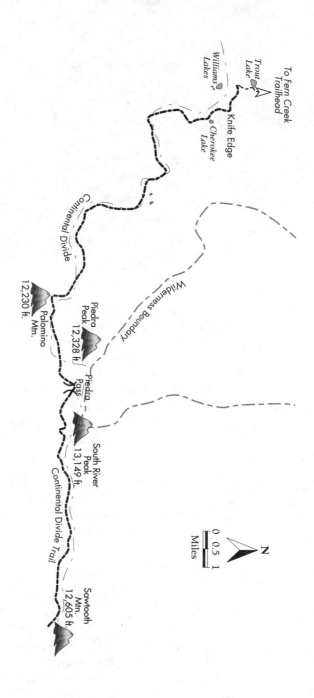

To Fern Creek Trailhead

Trout Lake

Williams Lakes

Knife Edge

Cherokee Lake

Continental Divide

Wilderness Boundary

Palomino Mtn.
12,230 ft.

Piedra Peak
12,328 ft.

Piedra Pass

South River Peak
13,149 ft.

Continental Divide Trail

Sawtooth Mtn.
12,605 ft.

N

0 0.5 1
Miles

Mike Vining on the CDT south of the Knife Edge and Cherokee Lake.

The hike: From the junction of the Continental Divide Trail (CDT) and the Highland Trail at Sawtooth Mountain, head northwest at a gradual descent. At 0.6 mile you'll see post-markers off to the left (south) that lead to Elk Creek, Beaver Meadow, and eventually Beaver Creek. To the right (north) you can see the Goose Creek drainage.

As you continue, you'll climb and descend at a gradual to moderate grade. You'll walk past wildflowers if you're there in mid- or late summer, and get wonderful views no matter what time of year. From 1.1 miles the trail is fairly level and open, allowing for grand views. You'll reach the junction for Sawtooth Trail (to the north) at 1.6 miles. The Goose Creek Trail, which leads to Goose Lake, is 2 miles from here.

After 2 miles you'll begin a moderately steep descent, reaching a mostly tree-covered saddle at 2.5 miles. In another 0.2 mile you'll see the remains of an old cabin (including a stove) on the left, just off the trail. Proceed through the trees from the saddle, climbing back out into the open at the 3-mile point. Cross another saddle, then climb up a steep grade. At 4 miles you'll cross yet another saddle to the north.

Next you'll descend at a moderate to easy grade, reaching a low point on a saddle at 4.6 miles. From here the trail follows the contour lines. You'll skirt a bench where there is a small creek and room to camp. You'll then begin a series of switchbacks to the top of a saddle at 6.5 miles and 12,860 feet above sea level. You'll get grand views of the wilderness and beyond from this point, the highest place along the Weminuche portion of the CDT. You'll see the Rio Grande Pyramid, the Grenadiers, and the Needles.

It's a short, steep descent to 6.7 miles and another saddle. Of course, grand views continue. After 7.1 miles you'll come to a junction with the Ivy

Creek Trail (Hike 27), going off to the right (north). This trail leads past the 13,149-foot summit of South River Peak, about 0.5 mile north. It also continues to Little Goose Lake, Goose Lake, and the Ivy Creek Trailhead.

The CDT stays to the left (west) at the junction. On it, you'll descend and cross a stream at 8.6 miles. Enter the trees just afterward. At 9.4 miles, you'll reach a junction with the Rainbow Trail, leading left (south) to the West Fork Trailhead. This is Piedra Pass, with abundant water and nice places to camp.

From Piedra Pass, the trail climbs easily to 9.6 miles and the Turkey Creek Trail to Turkey Lake. (Please note: There's a sign for the East Fork Piedra River.) The Turkey Creek Trail heads into the drainage to the south/southwest; post-markers mark the CDT, which runs parallel to the Turkey Creek Trail, but at a higher elevation.

You'll gradually climb to 9.7 miles and cross a stream. It's a moderate uphill to the 10-mile mark, where the CDT curves west. You'll hike mostly in the trees, crossing occasional meadows. You'll emerge into the open at 10.7 miles when you cross an immense talus slope. You'll alternately climb and descend, sometimes steeply, to the 13-mile point and the East Trout Creek Trail junction. Look for the CDT just up the hill.

Next you'll climb to meet the Middle Fork Trail; it's atop a plateau. At 14 miles you'll descend slightly through a boggy area. Then you'll follow post-markers to the edge of the basin, where you'll descend the easy to moderate grade. At 14.4 miles you'll begin a short, steep ascent to the top. You'll continue across sideslopes—some open, some covered with trees—throughout most of your journey to Trout Lake.

The trail climbs and descends in turn, reaching a wonderful little basin at 15.6 miles. Within the basin you'll find some little tarns. Look for places to camp in the nearby trees. Descend to 16 miles, then begin the same thing all over again—lots of ups and downs, sometimes in the woods, sometimes not, sometimes steep, sometimes not. You'll also tend to stay on top of the Continental Divide, though you will drop on the north and south sides at times.

At 18.1 miles there's a body of water on your right. It's a 300-foot descent to the lake, where you'll find places to camp. If you're looking for the Middle Fork Piedra River Trail, you can probably find it someplace in the area. I couldn't; it is almost impossible to detect from the CDT.

After 18.8 miles you'll emerge into the open, staying on the Continental Divide, continuing rollercoaster-like amid grand views. At one point you'll climb to 11,950 feet above sea level. At 20.1 miles you'll cross a saddle and get wonderful views all around. To the north, look into the Middle Trout Creek drainage; you may see a herd of elk.

Proceed along the exposed Continental Divide to 20.9 miles, then drop onto a saddle and a place where the CDT heads north. At 21.2 miles there's a trail heading left (south) to Palisade Meadows. Go straight ahead. After traversing the Continental Divide for another mile, you'll descend a sideslope where there is lots of vegetation, plus a stream crossing. You can see Cherokee Lake off to the north at 23.5 miles. A side trail descends a short distance to the lake, where there are wonderful views and places to camp in the spruce trees.

Beyond Cherokee Lake you'll head across open tundra, climbing to the rock promontory/sliver called the Knife Edge at 24.4 miles. There are incredible views from here. If you hit the wildflowers just right, you'll see an impressive display as you continue to Trout Lake. Continue west, hiking across the Knife Edge, which can be covered with slippery snow until mid-July or later. Descend to the Trout Lake/Williams Lakes Trails at 25.3 miles. The lakes are less than a mile away. Trout Lake is to the right (north), and Williams Lakes are to the left (south).

Camping: Big Meadows Campground is about 13 miles southwest of South Fork, off Big Meadow Reservoir Road (Forest Road 410). It's a fee area with drinking water and outhouses. Marshall Park Campground is 6.5 miles southwest of Creede, right off Colorado 149. It, too, is a fee area; facilities include water and outhouses.

38 Trout Lake to Weminuche Pass

Highlights:	Stunning views, high mountain lakes, abundant wildflowers. Wildlife, including bighorn sheep near Hossick Peak.
Distance:	19.5 miles one-way.
Difficulty:	Moderate to strenuous.
Elevation gain and loss:	+3,480 feet, -4,923 feet.
Maps:	USGS Little Squaw Creek, Granite Lake, Cimarrona Peak, and Weminuche Pass; Trails Illustrated Weminuche Wilderness.
Management:	Divide Ranger District, Rio Grande National Forest; Pagosa and Columbine Ranger Districts, San Juan National Forest.
Trail conditions:	The trail is easy to follow, but above treeline for some of the way; watch for late afternoon thunderstorms. Moderate use.

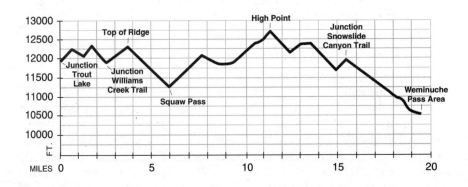

Trout Lake to Weminuche Pass

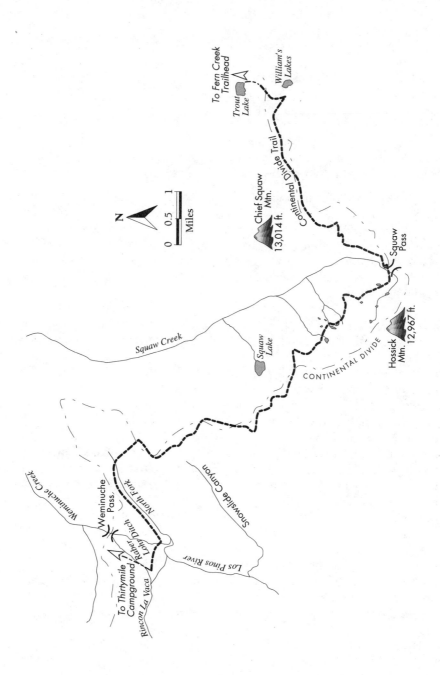

Finding the trailhead: You can access the Continental Divide Trail near Trout Lake from the Fern Creek Trailhead (see Hike 28); you'll add 12 miles to your hike.

The CDT near Weminuche Pass is accessible from Thirtymile Campground; see Hike 34 for more information.

Key points

0.0 (38.5)	Trout Lake Trail junction.
2.5 (41.0)	Williams Creek Trail junction.
3.6 (42.1)	Top of ridge.
5.9 (44.4)	Squaw Pass.
11.4 (49.9)	High point of this CDT section.
15.5 (54.0)	Snowslide Canyon Trail junction.
19.5 (58.0)	Pine River Trail near Weminuche Pass.

The hike: From the junction to the Trout Lake/Williams Lakes Trail, you'll be able to access the lakes easily. Trout Lake is 0.7 mile to the right (north), and Williams Lakes are 0.5 mile to the left (south). Continue west on the CDT from this junction, following post-markers across the tundra. I saw a ptarmigan and her babies in this area, as well as sulphur and fuchsia paintbrush, elephant head, marsh marigolds, bluebells, Colorado columbine, and many other flowers.

At 0.7 mile you'll reach the top of a ridge. You'll then descend to 1.3 miles and a narrow saddle. From here there are excellent views into the Little Squaw Creek drainage. Be sure to look for elk and wildflowers. You'll climb for the next 0.5 mile, staying near the top of the Continental Divide (mostly on the north side), then descend to 2.5 miles and the Williams Creek Trail. This is actually the junction with the trail that leads to the west fork of Williams Creek. There are a couple of little lakes here, and places to camp, too.

You'll climb again to 3.6 miles and the top of a ridge, just south of Chief Squaw Mountain. From here you can see west to the Needles, the Rio Grande Pyramid, The Window, and a whole lot more. Descend into the Squaw Creek drainage, dropping at a moderate, sometimes steep, grade, eventually reaching the trees at 4.7 miles. After 5 miles you'll parallel a pretty stream, crossing it at 5.1 miles. You'll see a trail—unsigned Squaw Creek Trail—merging from the right (south) at 5.6 miles; see Hike 31 for details on this route.

Continue left (south) along a talus slope. You'll reach the meadowy realm of Squaw Pass at 5.9 miles; there are places to camp in the trees. Beyond the pass, you'll begin a short, steep climb to the bench to the west. You'll hike in the trees, then switchback up at 6.1 miles. The trail exits the trees at 6.6 miles, where there's a stream. The grade becomes more gradual here. After 7.3 miles there's a lake on the right; you may spot a nice place to camp in the trees.

Hike another 0.5 mile, then begin a steep descent to another basin which you'll reach at 8.5 miles. You'll walk past a number of small lakes before crossing a stream at 9.1 miles. Next you'll climb a moderate to steep grade to 10.7 miles and a ridge offering lots of wildflowers and more grand views.

Mike Vining on the Continental Divide Trail.

Continue climbing to 10.9 miles; from this point, you'll be able to see Squaw Lake on the right. After 11.4 miles you'll reach the highest point on this section of the CDT at 12,780 feet above sea level. The views are endless.

The trail descends at a steep grade to 11.8 miles and the Squaw Lake Trail junction. Continue on, dropping into a low part of the basin before climbing a steep slope. You'll reach the top of the next ridge at 13 miles. Next you'll hike across a wide, high plateau where grand views remain.

It's a fairly level hike across the plateau. You'll then begin a moderate, sometimes steep, descent, still hiking in the open. At 14.9 miles you'll pass the head of Snowslide Canyon. You'll see many ponds in the area. Begin a moderate climb at 15.2 miles. Then, at 15.5 miles, you'll reach the trail's junction with the Snowslide Canyon Trail. This is also the top of the ridge.

A steep, then later moderate, descent leads down into the trees at 15.7 miles. Along the way you'll emerge for a nice view of The Window, the Rio Grande Pyramid, and other formations. At 16.5 miles you'll cross the North Fork Pine River. There are places to camp in this area, and lots of wildflowers in season. You'll cross the river again soon after.

The route descends moderately to the trees at 18.3 miles, then continues to Fuchs Diversion Ditch at 18.7 miles. You'll reach the meadow near Weminuche Pass just beyond the ditch. Look for places to camp in the trees. The CDT crosses the meadow, following post-markers and jumping a canal at 19.1 miles. It meets the Pine River (Los Pinos) Trail, which is unsigned, at 19.5 miles. Follow post-markers to take the CDT west from here. There are places to camp in the trees. At an elevation of 10,527 feet, this is the lowest part of the CDT in the Weminuche.

Camping: Marshall Park Campground is 6.5 miles southwest of Creede, right off Colorado 149. It's a fee area; facilities include water and outhouses. Thirtymile Campground is 30 miles southwest of Creede off Rio Grande Reservoir Road (Forest Road 520). It, too, is a fee area; facilities include water and outhouses.

39 Weminuche Pass to Stony Pass

Highlights: Spectacular views, high mountain lakes. Wildlife and wildflowers.
Distance: 27.7 miles one-way.
Difficulty: Moderate to strenuous.
Elevation gain and loss: +6,630 feet, -4,603 feet.
Maps: USGS Weminuche Pass, Rio Grande Pyramid, Storm King Peak, and Howardsville; Trails Illustrated Weminuche Wilderness.
Management: Divide Ranger District, Rio Grande National Forest; Columbine Ranger District, San Juan National Forest.
Trail conditions: The trail is easy to follow in most places, difficult in others, and nearly nonexistent near Stony Pass. The CDT is above treeline much of the way, so watch for late afternoon thunderstorms. Snow can be deep in places, as late as July. Light use near Stony Pass; heavy use at Weminuche Pass.

Finding the trailhead: The northernmost section of the Weminuche portion of the Continental Divide Trail is found at Stony Pass, accessible from Silverton. From the junction of U.S. Highway 550 and Colorado 110 at the southwest end of town, drive northeast on CO 110 (Greene Street). After 1 mile go right (east) on CO 110. The road is paved for the first 2 miles, then turns to maintained gravel. After another 2.1 miles turn right (south) on San Juan County Road 4 (some maps show this as Forest Road 589) toward Stony Pass.

After an additional 1.7 miles the road forks again. Keep left (southeast) on San Juan County Road 3 (Forest Road 737) for another 4.1 miles to the top of Stony Pass (elevation +12,588 feet). The trailhead is a couple hundred yards east of the pass, near the remains of an old cabin on the right (south) side of the road.

Because the 2+ miles of the CDT south of Stony Pass are hard to find and follow, I recommend an alternate route: begin and end this section by hiking in or out of the Cunningham Gulch Trail (Hike 1). It is easier to follow, and you don't need a 4-wheel-drive vehicle to get there.

The CDT near Weminuche Pass is accessible from Thirtymile Campground; see Hike 34 for trailhead information.

Key points
0.0 (58.0)	Pine River Trail junction near Weminuche Pass.
3.3 (61.3)	Trail 564 junction.
5.6 (63.6)	East Ute Creek Trail junction.
7.7 (65.7)	Junction atop ridge.
9.5 (67.5)	Rock Lake Trail junction.
11.7 (69.7)	Middle Ute Lake Trail junction.
13.6 (71.6)	West Ute Lake Trail junction.

14.9 (72.9)   Nebo Pass.
18.1 (76.1)   Hunchback Pass.
21.3 (79.3)   Elk Creek Trail junction.
25.3 (83.3)   Cunningham Gulch Trail junction.
27.7 (85.7)   Stony Pass.

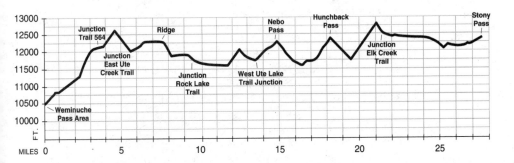

The hike: From the junction of the Pine River (Los Pinos) Trail and the CDT near Weminuche Pass, follow the CDT post-markers to where you'll ford the Rincon La Vaca. Just beyond this river, you'll begin a steep climb through the trees. After 0.5 mile you'll enter a meadow, paralleling Rincon La Vaca. There are nice places to camp here, with good views of The Window and Rio Grande Pyramid.

You'll cross several little streams as you hike to the west end of the meadow, where you'll begin a steep climb. At 1.1 miles you'll enter the trees; there's a pond on the left just beyond. After 1.6 miles you'll descend a bit, switching between meadow and trees as you parallel a stream. Begin climbing a very steep slope at 2.1 miles. The trail skirts a talus slope, with a pretty waterfall off to the side at 2.3 miles.

At 2.5 miles you'll come to a fork: One trail heads southwest, the other northwest. Go left (southwest) and continue the steep climb for another half a mile or so. At 2.9 miles the trail eases, climbing more gradually. Nice views of The Window and the Rio Grande Pyramid continue as you ascend through willows.

At 3.2 miles you'll cross a stream. Soon afterward, at 3.3 miles, Trail 564 joins the CDT from the right. This trail is unsigned, but post-markers point the way up the ridge to the northeast. You continue on the main route, crossing nearly flat terrain and streams at 3.4 and 3.7 miles. Just after the last crossing you'll reach a small lake, which mirrors The Window. There are nice places to camp in the area, but it's wide open and exposed. (Note: Topographic maps show the CDT passing by the south end of the lake when it fact it comes in from the northeast.)

From this mirror lake, you'll climb at a gradual to moderate grade to a ridgetop at 4.6 miles. You'll get a nice view into the Ute drainages from here, with an abundance of wildflowers to keep you occupied on the descent. The drop is a moderate one, but the grade steepens as you near the head of the East Ute Creek drainage.

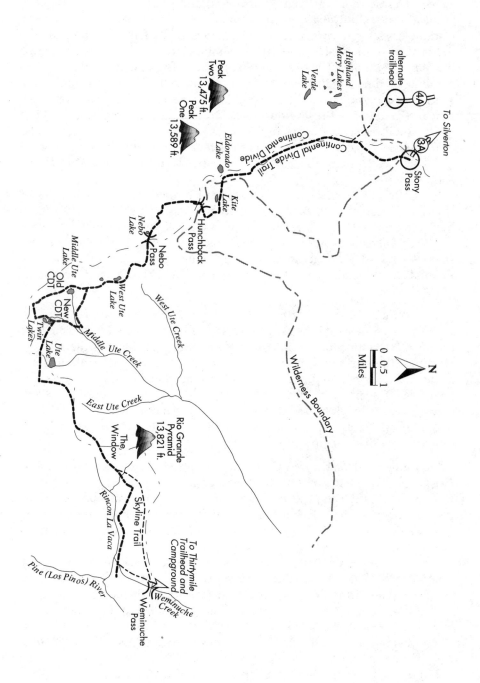

You'll reach the East Ute Creek Trail junction at 5.6 miles. Follow the rock cairns to a junction where a spur trail heads left (southeast) to the Rincon La Osa. Continue right (northwest) on the CDT.

Next, you'll climb at a gradual to moderate grade to a stream at 6.3 miles. Continue to a nice view from the ridge down to Ute Lake. You'll regain the top of the Continental Divide after 7.5 miles. Proceed along the ridge to a junction at 7.7 miles. Here, yet another trail heads east to Rincon La Osa. To continue on the CDT, hike southwest and drop to the Ute Lakes area. (Once again the topographic map is in error.) You'll descend steeply to a trail junction at 8 miles. Take the left (northwest) fork and head directly toward Ute Lake. You'll descend steeply to 8.2 miles and the junction to Flint Lakes Trail on the left (south). Just beyond this crossroads is another branch of the Ute Lake Trail; it's to the right and northwest. Keep straight and to the southwest.

Pass Ute Lake, where camping sites are limited due to thick willows. Now you'll climb at an easy to moderate grade for a short distance, then begin dropping. At 8.7 miles there's a nice view of the basin ahead. You can see Twin Lakes and several high peaks after 9 miles. You'll then begin a steep descent to a fork at 9.5 miles. Keep going straight (north) on the Continental Divide Trail. Go left (southwest) to reach Rock Lake and the Middle Ute Lake Trail.

Special Note: As this book was going to press the CDT was rerouted, as noted on the enclosed map. If you'd like to hike the old CDT, which stays true to the Continental Divide but adds another 1.4 miles to the hike, go west past the north end of Twin Lakes, then climb the moderate to steep slope to the Rock Trail junction. From there head north on the Middle Ute Lake Trail, traversing a sideslope bursting with summer wildflowers. Once the trail was difficult to find due to thick willows, but the trail was cleared in summer 1998 and is now a pleasure to hike. You'll reach the 11.7-mile junction mentioned below after another 2.2 miles.

Continue north on the new CDT, descending to the junction of the Middle Ute Creek Trail at 10.6 miles. Head west from here, climbing a fairly steep trail to the Middle Ute Lake Trail junction at 11.7 miles. Post-markers show you the way to both trails. You can see back to the Rio Grande Pyramid and The Window from here. It's a moderate to steep climb to the top of a ridge at 12.3 miles. Grand views continue there.

Descend the moderate to steep trail, passing a little lake on the left at 12.6 miles. Reach West Ute Lake after 12.9 miles. Remember that you must camp at least 300 feet from the lake; the best places are on the northeast side.

You'll reach the West Ute Creek Trail at 13.6 miles. At this junction, the West Ute Creek Trail heads straight (north), while the CDT goes left (northwest). Just beyond the junction, you'll cross a stream. (Note: The CDT over Nebo Pass is not shown on topographic maps.) Hike in the trees at first, then out in the open where there is an abundance of wildflowers.

The trail ascends at an easy to moderate grade to 13.7 miles, where you'll cross a creek. It then climbs at a steep—sometimes very steep—grade, cross-

Donna Ikenberry and Mike Vining on the Continental Divide Trail. The Window in back.

ing the most northerly of two creeks at 14.4 miles. Pass a little lake on the left. At 14.7 miles, you'll cross another creek. You'll then reach the top of Nebo Pass at 12,450 feet above sea level. There are wonderful views of the Grenadiers from here. For an even better view, descend just a bit for a fantastic view of Nebo Lake with the peaks in the background.

From Nebo Pass, descend moderately to 15.6 miles, where you'll cross yet another stream. Now a very steep switchback leads down to 15.7 miles and the crossing of Nebo Creek. Almost immediately after crossing the creek you'll cross again, now hiking the south side of Nebo Creek.

After 15.9 miles the trail eases up some, and the nice views continue. But the trail soon becomes difficult to find. It follows Nebo Creek (actually using the creekbed as a trail) for 100 yards or so, then crosses to the north side of the creek and heads into the trees. At 16.3 miles it moves away from Nebo Creek, descending moderately to an unsigned junction with the Vallecito Creek Trail. If you need a place to camp head down (south) the Vallecito Creek Trail. There's a place not far away in the trees, with water available from nearby Nebo Creek.

You'll see lots of willows, wildflowers, and other vegetation as you hike north up Vallecito Creek. It's a steep climb to 17 miles, where you cross Vallecito Creek. Cross several side streams and the headwaters of Vallecito, then climb a steep grade to the top of Hunchback Pass at 18.1 miles. This pass sits at 12,493 feet above sea level, reaching into the heavens. From here you can see south to the Guardian, the most prominent peak in view, and farther south into the Needle Mountains.

At this point, you'll pass out of the wilderness. You'll descend a moderate to steep slope, while wonderful views continue. Cross several streams and pass some old mining remains en route to a junction with a four-wheel-drive road at 19.6 miles. There's a trail register here; be sure to sign in or out.

To continue on the CDT, hike left (west) and up the four-wheel-drive road. It's a steep climb up to Kite Lake at 20 miles. You'll find an old mining cabin and a couple of mineshafts, but not much in the way of flat camping spots. Just prior to reaching the lake, look for a rock cairn marking a trail off to the right (north). Climb the steep (sometimes very steep) grade, crossing a stream en route to the 12,800-foot level at 20.9 miles. You are standing on the Continental Divide, and there's a grand view of Eldorado Lake, with Peak Two behind it. You can also see the Elk Creek drainage and lakes north of it.

Turn right (north) on the CDT. You'll reach a high point of 12,840 feet, then soon begin a short but steep descent over rocky terrain. You'll meet the Elk Creek Trail at 21.3 miles. Hike another 0.3 mile to another junction at 21.6 miles. Here the Colorado Trail takes off to the right (east); you go left (northwest) on the CDT.

Follow post-markers to 21.7 miles, then stay north past some pretty little lakes. Rock cairns lead the way as you roll up and down to the 23.5-mile point. Look for two rock cairns here, one to the west and the other to the east. Follow the trail that passes between the two.

At 23.8 miles you'll reach the unsigned junction with the trail to Verde Lakes. The terrain still rolls as you continue to a small lake on the left at 24.3 miles. Descend steeply to a small lake on the right. After 25.3 miles, look for two post-markers and large rock cairn off to the right. While the most defined trail heads straight, the unsigned CDT is visible to the northeast. If you'd like to begin or end this segment at Cunningham Gulch, stay on the main trail, which is the unsigned Cunningham Gulch Trail. It descends 1,380 feet and ends 2.6 miles later at the Highland Mary Lakes Trailhead; see Hike 1 for details.

The last portion of the CDT is tough to follow because it is difficult to find the trail. Although we managed to find Stony Pass (it's easy to see where you're going in this part of the country), there were many steep ravines that made getting there difficult. My best advice is to aim northeast at this point, hiking around the east side of the Continental Divide. You'll come to a faint trail after 0.3 mile or so. Head east, going up and around the ridge. You'll see other trails heading up the ridge; don't take these, since they are old sheep trails.

As you round the ridge, the trail becomes obscure once again. Travel in a northeasterly direction, eventually crossing a stream at about 26.4 miles. Continue heading north to a post-marker and a CDT sign at 26.5 miles. (If you find this sign, you have it made!) At 27 miles there's a post-marker. Continue to 27.3 miles and a creek crossing. Pass the cabin remains and reach the trailhead at Stony Pass at 27.7 miles. If you've hiked the whole CDT route in the Weminuche, you've come 85.7 miles!

Camping: Silverton offers several private campgrounds. The public Thirtymile Campground is 30 miles southwest of Creede off Rio Grande Reservoir Road (Forest Road 520). It's a fee area; facilities include water and outhouses.

Appendix A: For More Information

American Hiking Society
P.O. Box 20160
Washington, DC 20041
(301) 565-6704
(301) 565-6714 fax

Bayfield Chamber of Commerce
1327 U.S. Highway 160B
Bayfield, CO 81122
(970) 884-9782

Colorado Mountain Club
2530 West Alameda Avenue
Denver, CO 80219
(303) 922-8315

Columbine Ranger District
San Juan National Forest
Bayfield Office
P.O. Box 349
Bayfield, CO 81122
(970) 884-2512

Columbine Ranger District
San Juan National Forest
Durango Office
701 Camino Del Rio
Durango, CO 81301
(970) 247-4874

Continental Divide Trail Alliance
P.O. Box 628
Pine, CO 80470
(303) 838-3760
website: www.CDTrail.org

Continental Divide Trail Society
3704 North Charles Street #601
Baltimore, MD 21218-2300
(410) 235-9610
website: www.gorp.com/cdts/

Creede-Mineral County Chamber of
  Commerce
Creede Avenue
Creede, CO 81130
(719) 658-2374

Divide Ranger District
Rio Grande National Forest
Creede Office
P.O. Box 270
Creede, CO 81130
(719) 658-2556

Durango Chamber Resort
  Association
P.O. Box 2587
111 South Camino Del Rio
Durango, CO 81302
(970) 247-0312
(970) 385-7884 fax
e-mail: durango@frontier.net.

Durango & Silverton Narrow Gauge
  Railroad
(970) 247-2733 or (888) 872-4607

Pagosa Springs Chamber of
  Commerce
402 San Juan Street
Pagosa Springs, CO 81147
(970) 264-4625 or (970) 264-2360

Pagosa Ranger District
San Juan National Forest
P.O. Box 310
Pagosa Springs, CO 81147
(970) 264-2268

San Juan Mountains Association
P.O. Box 2261
Durango, CO 81302
(970) 385-1210
(970) 385-1243 fax

Sierra Club
Rocky Mountain Chapter
2239 East Colfax Avenue
Denver, CO 80206
(303) 321-8292

Silverton Chamber of Commerce
P.O. Box 565
Silverton, CO 81433
(970) 387-5654 or (800) 752-4494
website: www.silverton.org

South Fork Chamber of Commerce
P.O. Box 116
South Fork, CO 81154
(719) 873-5512
website: www.@southfork.org

Maps

Trails Illustrated Maps
P.O Box 4357
Evergreen, CO 80439-3746
(303) 670-3457 or (800) 962-1643

United States Geological Survey
(USGS)
Western Distribution Branch
P.O. Box 25286
Denver Federal Center
Denver, CO 80225

Some specialty backpacking stores
and sporting goods stores also carry
USGS maps.

Weather and road information
Call (970) 247-3355.

In case of emergency
Call 911 or the sheriff's office nearest to the emergency.

Near Durango (970) 247-4722
Near Southfork (719) 657-4000
Near Bayfield (970) 247-1155
Near Pagosa Springs (970) 264-2131
Near Creede (719) 658-2600

Appendix B: Further Reading

Berger, Karen. *Hiking and Backpacking: A Complete Guide.* New York: W.
    W. Norton & Co., 1994.

Fletcher, Colin. *The Complete Walker III.* New York: Alfred A. Knopf, 1984.

Harmon, Will. *Wild Country Companion.* Helena, Mont.: Falcon Publish-
    ing, 1994.

Hart, John. *Walking Softly in the Wilderness.* San Francisco: Sierra Club
    Books, 1984.

Ormes, Robert. *Guide to the Colorado Mountains.* Denver: The Colorado
Mountain Club, 1992.

Randall, Glenn. *The Modern Backpacker's Handbook.* New York: Lyons &
    Burford Publishers, 1994.

Wolf, James R. *Guide to the Continental Divide Trail. Volume 5, Southern
    Colorado.* Bethesda, MD: Continental Divide Trail Society, 1986.

Appendix C: Hiker Checklist

Don't forget essential equipment—always prepare a checklist before leaving home. You may not need everything on the following list, but it'll help ensure that you've packed all the necessary gear for your trip.

- ☐ Day pack and/or backpack
- ☐ Sleeping bag
- ☐ Air mattress or foam pad
- ☐ Ground sheet and/or tarp
- ☐ Dependable tent
- ☐ Sturdy footwear
- ☐ Lightweight camp shoes or sandals
- ☐ Sunglasses
- ☐ Sunscreen
- ☐ Lip balm
- ☐ Insect repellent
- ☐ Mosquito headnet
- ☐ Maps and compass
- ☐ Matches in waterproof container
- ☐ Toilet paper
- ☐ Lightweight plastic trowel
- ☐ Pocket knife
- ☐ First-aid kit
- ☐ Survival kit
- ☐ Flashlight with fresh batteries and spare bulb candle
- ☐ 50 feet of nylon parachute cord
- ☐ Extra stuffsacks for bear-bagging food
- ☐ Water filter
- ☐ One-quart water container(s)
- ☐ One-gallon water container (collapsible) for camp use
- ☐ Platypus bottle (for use as a hot water bottle)
- ☐ Plastic bags (for trash)
- ☐ Biodegradable soap
- ☐ Towel
- ☐ Toothbrush
- ☐ Cookware
- ☐ Spoon and fork
- ☐ Camp stove and extra fuel
- ☐ Pot scrubber
- ☐ Enough food, plus a little extra
- ☐ Camera, film, lenses, filters, tripod
- ☐ Binoculars
- ☐ Waterproof cover for pack
- ☐ Dependable rain parka

- ❏ Windproof parka
- ❏ Thermal underwear (polypropylene or capilene is best)
- ❏ Shorts and/or long pants
- ❏ Wool cap or balaclava
- ❏ Wool shirt and/or sweater
- ❏ Jacket or parka
- ❏ Extra socks
- ❏ Underwear
- ❏ Mittens or gloves
- ❏ Watch
- ❏ Sewing kit
- ❏ Hat
- ❏ Paperback book
- ❏ Magazine

Trail Finder Table

	EASY	MODERATE	DIFFICULT

Backcountry Lakes	None	4 Crater Lake
		7 Lime Mesa
		19 Turkey Creek Trail
		24 Hunters Lake Loop
		34 Ute Creek
			2 Highland Mary Lakes
			8 Endlich Mesa/
			   Burnt Timber
			   Shuttle-Loop
			10 Pine River/Flint
			   Creek Semi-Loop
			12 Divide Lakes
			13 Granite Lake
			15 Williams Creek to
			   Williams Lake
			18 Fourmile Lake Loop
			21 South Fork/
			   Archuleta Lake
			   Semi-Loop
			27 Ivy Creek Trail
			28 Fern Creek to
			   Trout Lake
			29 Ruby Lakes/Red
			   Lakes Semi-Loop
			30 Jumper Lake
			36–39 Continental
			   Divide Trail

Waterfalls	17 Piedra Falls	None	9 Vallecito Creek Trail 11 Pine River Trail 18 Fourmile Lake Loop

Alpine Country	None	3 Molas Trail
		7 Lime Mesa
		25 Highland Trail
		31 Squaw Pass
		32 Weminuche Pass
		33 The Window
		34 Ute Creek
		   Semi-Loop
		35 Starvation Pass
			2 Highland Mary
			   Lakes
			5 Elk Park/
			   Chicago Basin
			   Shuttle-Loop
			8 Endlich Mesa/Burnt
			   Timber Shuttle-Loop
			10 Pine River/
			   Flint Creek
			   Semi-Loop
			15 Williams Creek
			   to Williams Lake

EASY	MODERATE	DIFFICULT
Alpine Country continued		21 South Fork/ Archuleta Lake Semi-Loop 26 Fisher Mountain 27 Ivy Creek Trail 28 Fern Creek to Trout Lake 29 Ruby Lakes/Red Lakes Semi-Loop 36–39 Continental Divide Trail

Author's Favorites

FOR PHOTOGRAPHY
2 Highland Mary Lakes
5 Elk Park/Chicago Basin Shuttle-Loop
7 Lime Mesa
8 Endlich Mesa/Burnt Timber Shuttle-Loop
22 Hope Creek Trail
25 Highland Trail
29 Ruby Lakes/Red Lakes Semi-Loop
33 The Window
34 Ute Creek Semi-Loop
35 Starvation Pass
36–39 Continental Divide Trail

FOR HIGH-ALTITUDE SCENERY
2 Highland Mary Lakes
5 Elk Park/Chicago Basin Shuttle-Loop
7 Lime Mesa
8 Endlich Mesa/Burnt Timber Shuttle-Loop
25 Highland Trail
26 Fisher Mountain
29 Ruby Lakes/Red Lakes Semi-Loop
33 The Window
35 Starvation Pass
36–39 Continental Divide Trail

FOR WILDLIFE
5 Elk Park/Chicago Basin Shuttle-Loop
18 Fourmile Lake Loop
19 Turkey Creek Trail
25 Highland Trail
29 Ruby Lakes/Red Lakes Semi-Loop
31 Squaw Pass
36–39 Continental Divide Trail

FOR WILDFLOWERS
1 Cunningham Gulch
2 Highland Mary Lakes
5 Elk Park/Chicago Basin Shuttle-Loop
7 Lime Mesa
8 Endlich Mesa/Burnt Timber Shuttle-Loop
25 Highland Trail
26 Fisher Mountain
27 Ivy Creek Trail
35 Starvation Pass
36–39 Continental Divide Trail

FOR AN EASY DAY HIKE
7 Lime Mesa (to Dollar Lake)

9 Vallecito Creek Trail (first few miles)
11 Pine River Trail (first few miles)
17 Piedra Falls
21 South Fork/Archuleta Lake Semi-Loop
(first few miles)

FOR A MODERATE DAY HIKE
7 Lime Mesa
22 Hope Creek Trail
32 Weminuche Pass
35 Starvation Pass

FOR A LONG, HARD DAY HIKE
2 Highland Mary Lakes
16 Palisade Meadows
18 Fourmile Lake Loop
26 Fisher Mountain
33 The Window

FOR THE FIRST NIGHT EVER IN THE WILDERNESS
9 Vallecito Creek Trail
11 Pine River Trail
24 Hunters Lake Loop

FOR A MODERATE OVERNIGHTER
4 Crater Lake
7 Lime Mesa
27 Ivy Creek Trail
32 Weminuche Pass

FOR A MODERATE OVERNIGHTER OF TWO NIGHTS OR MORE
31 Squaw Pass
34 Ute Creek Semi-Loop

FOR A STRENUOUS BACKPACK OF SEVERAL DAYS OR MORE
5 Elk Park/Chicago Basin Shuttle-Loop
8 Endlich Mesa/Burnt Timber Shuttle-Loop
10 Pine River/Flint Creek Semi-Loop
29 Ruby Lakes/Red Lakes Semi-Loop
36–39 Continental Divide Trail

FOR BASE CAMP OPTIONS
4 Crater Lake
7 Lime Mesa
14 East Fork Weminuche Trail
34 Ute Creek Semi-Loop

Index

Page numbers in *italic* type refer to photos.
Page numbers in **bold** type refer to maps.

About the Author

Donna Ikenberry is a full-time, freelance photojournalist who travels year-round. She has called her 30-foot fifth-wheel trailer "home" for more than 15 years.

Donna has written six Oregon hiking guides: *Hiking Oregon, Color Guide to Oregon's Wilderness Areas, Southern Oregon Wilderness Areas, Eastern Oregon Wilderness Areas, Central Oregon Wilderness Areas,* and *Northern Oregon Wilderness Areas.* An avid bicyclist, she is also the author of two bicycling guidebooks, *Bicycling the Atlantic Coast* and *Bicycling Coast to Coast.* She is also the author of *Oregon's Outback,* an auto tour guide to southeastern Oregon.

In addition to books, she has written nearly 500 articles on various topics. Thousands of her photographs have graced the covers and pages of many magazines, books, postcards, advertisements, videos, posters, and calendars.

On a special note, just before this book went to press, Donna married Mike Vining, a retired U.S. Army Sergeant major who is also an avid mountaineer and climber.

The Wilderness Society

THE WILDERNESS SOCIETY'S ROOTS

When their car came to a screeching halt somewhere outside of Knoxville, Tennessee, the passengers were in hot debate over plans for a new conservation group. The men got out of the car and climbed an embankment where they sat and argued over the philosophy and definition of the new organization.

Three months later, in January 1935, the group met again in Washington, D. C. Participants in the meeting included Robert Sterling Yard, publicist for the National Park Service; Benton MacKaye, the "Father of the Appalachian Trail"; and Robert Marshall, chief of recreation and lands for the USDA Forest Service. "All we desire to save from invasion," they declared, "is that extremely minor fraction of outdoor America which yet remains free from mechanical sights and sounds and smells." For a name, they finally settled on The Wilderness Society.

Among the co-founders was Aldo Leopold, a wildlife ecologist at the University of Wisconsin. In Leopold's view, The Wilderness Society would help form the cornerstone of a movement needed to save America's vanishing wilderness. It took nearly 30 years, but President Lyndon B. Johnson finally signed The Wilderness Act of 1964 into law September 3rd, in the rose garden of the White House.

THE WILDERNESS SOCIETY TODAY

The founders called the organization The Wilderness Society, and they put out an urgent call, as we do today, for "spirited people who will fight for the freedom of the wilderness." Today, Americans enjoy some 104 million acres of protected wilderness, due in large part to the efforts of The Wilderness Society. The Wilderness Society is a nonprofit organization devoted to protecting America's wilderness and developing a nation-wide network of wild lands through public education, scientific analysis and activism. The organization's goal is to ensure that future generations will enjoy the clean air and water, wildlife, beauty and opportunity for renewal provided by pristine forests, mountains, rivers and deserts. You can help protect American wildlands by becoming a Wilderness Society Member. Here are three ways you can join: **Telephone: 1-800-THE-WILD; E-mail: member@tws.org or visit the web site: www.wilderness.org; Write:The Wilderness Society, Attention: Membership, 900 17th Street Northwest, Washington, D.C. 20006.**

FALCON GUIDES ® Leading the Way™

FALCON GUIDES ® are available for where-to-go hiking, mountain biking, rock climbing, walking, scenic driving, fishing, rockhounding, paddling, birding, wildlife viewing, and camping. We also have FalconGuides on essential outdoor skills and subjects and field identification. The following titles are currently available, but this list grows every year. For a free catalog with a complete list of titles, call FALCON toll-free at 1-800-582-2665.

BEST EASY DAY HIKES SERIES
Beartooths
Canyonlands & Arches
Cape Cod
Colorado Springs
Glacier & Wateron Lakes
Grand Canyon
Grand Staircase-Escalante and
   the Glen Canyon Region
Grand Teton
Lake Tahoe
Mount Rainier
Mount St. Helens
North Cascades
Olympics
Salt Lake City
Shenandoah
Yellowstone

12 SHORT HIKES SERIES
California
San Diego Coast
San Diego Mountains
San Francisco Bay Area-Coastal
San Francisco Bay Area-East Bay
San Francisco Bay Area-North Bay
San Francisco Bay Area-South Bay
Colorado
Aspen
Boulder
Denver Foothills Central
Denver Foothills North
Denver Foothills South
Rocky Mountain National Park-Estes Park
Rocky Mountain National Park-Grand Lake
Steamboat Springs
Summit County
Vail
Washington
Mount Rainier National Park-Paradise
Mount Rainier National Park-Sunrise

■ *To order any of these books, check with your local bookseller*
*or call FALCON ® at **1-800-582-2665**.*
Visit us on the world wide web at:
www.FalconOutdoors.com

FALCON®

FALCON GUIDES ® Leading the Way

FIELD GUIDES

Bitterroot: Montana State Flower
Canyon Country Wildflowers
Central Rocky Mountains
   Wildflowers
Great Lakes Berry Book
New England Berry Book
Ozark Wildflowers
Pacific Northwest Berry Book
Plants of Arizona
Rare Plants of Colorado
Rocky Mountain Berry Book
Scats & Tracks of the Pacific
   Coast States
Scats & Tracks of the
   Rocky Mountains
Southern Rocky Mountain
   Wildflowers
Tallgrass Prairie Wildflowers
Western Trees
Wildflowers of Southwestern
   Utah
Willow Bark and Rosehips

FISHING GUIDES

Fishing Alaska
Fishing the Beartooths
Fishing Florida
Fishing Glacier National Park
Fishing Maine
Fishing Montana
Fishing Wyoming
Fishing Yellowstone
   National Park

ROCKHOUNDING GUIDES

Rockhounding Arizona
Rockhounding California
Rockhounding Colorado
Rockhounding Montana
Rockhounding Nevada
Rockhound's Guide to New
   Mexico
Rockhounding Texas
Rockhounding Utah
Rockhounding Wyoming

MORE GUIDEBOOKS

Backcountry Horseman's
   Guide to Washington
Camping California's
   National Forests
Exploring Canyonlands &
   Arches National Parks
Exploring Hawaii's Parklands
Exploring Mount Helena
Exploring Southern California
   Beaches
Recreation Guide to WA
   National Forests
Touring California & Nevada
   Hot Springs
Touring Colorado Hot Springs
Touring Montana & Wyoming
   Hot Springs
Trail Riding Western
   Montana
Wild Country Companion
Wilderness Directory
Wild Montana
Wild Utah

BIRDING GUIDES

Birding Minnesota
Birding Montana
Birding Northern California
Birding Texas
Birding Utah

PADDLING GUIDES

Floater's Guide to Colorado
Paddling Minnesota
Paddling Montana
Paddling Okefenokee
Paddling Oregon
Paddling Yellowstone & Grand
   Teton National Parks

HOW-TO GUIDES

Avalanche Aware
Backpacking Tips
Bear Aware
Desert Hiking Tips
Hiking with Dogs
Leave No Trace
Mountain Lion Alert
Reading Weather
Route Finding
Using GPS
Wilderness First Aid
Wilderness Survival

WALKING

Walking Colorado Springs
Walking Denver
Walking Portland
Walking St. Louis
Walking Virginia Beach

■ *To order any of these books, check with your local bookseller
or call FALCON* ® *at* **1-800-582-2665**.
Visit us on the world wide web at:
www.FalconOutdoors.com

FALCON®

FALCONGUIDES ® Leading the Way™

FALCONGUIDES ® are available for where-to-go hiking, mountain biking, rock climbing, walking, scenic driving, fishing, rockhounding, paddling, birding, wildlife viewing, and camping. We also have FalconGuides on essential outdoor skills and subjects and field identification. The following titles are currently available, but this list grows every year. For a free catalog with a complete list of titles, call FALCON toll-free at 1-800-582-2665.

HIKING GUIDES

Hiking Alaska
Hiking Arizona
Hiking Arizona's Cactus Country
Hiking the Beartooths
Hiking Big Bend National Park
Hiking the Bob Marshall Country
Hiking California
Hiking California's Desert Parks
Hiking Carlsbad Caverns
   and Guadalupe Mtns. National Parks
Hiking Colorado
Hiking Colorado, Vol.II
Hiking Colorado's Summits
Hiking Colorado's Weminuche Wilderness
Hiking the Columbia River Gorge
Hiking Florida
Hiking Georgia
Hiking Glacier & Waterton Lakes National Parks
Hiking Grand Canyon National Park
Hiking Grand Staircase-Escalante/Glen Canyon
Hiking Grand Teton National Park
Hiking Great Basin National Park
Hiking Hot Springs in the Pacific Northwest
Hiking Idaho
Hiking Maine
Hiking Michigan
Hiking Minnesota
Hiking Montana
Hiking Mount Rainier National Park
Hiking Mount St. Helens
Hiking Nevada
Hiking New Hampshire

Hiking New Mexico
Hiking New York
Hiking North Carolina
Hiking the North Cascades
Hiking Northern Arizona
Hiking Olympic National Park
Hiking Oregon
Hiking Oregon's Eagle Cap Wilderness
Hiking Oregon's Mount Hood/Badger Creek
Hiking Oregon's Three Sisters Country
Hiking Pennsylvania
Hiking Shenandoah National Park
Hiking the Sierra Nevada
Hiking South Carolina
Hiking South Dakota's Black Hills Country
Hiking Southern New England
Hiking Tennessee
Hiking Texas
Hiking Utah
Hiking Utah's Summits
Hiking Vermont
Hiking Virginia
Hiking Washington
Hiking Wyoming
Hiking Wyoming's Cloud Peak Wilderness
Hiking Wyoming's Wind River Range
Hiking Yellowstone National Park
Hiking Zion & Bryce Canyon National Parks
The Trail Guide to Bob Marshall Country
Wild Country Companion
Wild Montana
Wild Utah

■ *To order any of these books, check with your local bookseller or call FALCON ® at **1-800-582-2665**.*
Visit us on the world wide web at:
www.FalconOutdoors.com

FALCON®